# DECREES

## AND

# AFFIRMATIONS

## FOR

# Prosperity

**sound** wisdom.
*Because Your Success Matters*

# DAILY DECREES AND AFFIRMATIONS FOR

## Prosperity

### 90 Days to Overcome Your Limiting Beliefs

## FLORENCE SCOVEL SHINN

Content derived from:

The Word Is Your Wand, first published in 1928 by Florence Scovel Shinn.

The Game of Life and How to Play It, first published in 1925 by Florence Scovel Shinn.

Reprint edition by Sound Wisdom, 2019, as The Game of Life and How to Play It.

ISBN 13 TP: 978-1-64095-515-8

ISBN 13 eBook: 978-1-64095-516-5

1 2 3 4 5 6 7 8 / 28 27 26 25 24

# Contents

Foreword . . . . . . . . . . . . . . . . . . . . . . . . . . . . . . . 11

1  The Word's Power . . . . . . . . . . . . . . . . . . . . . 13

2  The Power of Your Words . . . . . . . . . . . . . . . 16

3  Truth Sets You Free . . . . . . . . . . . . . . . . . . . . 18

4  An Open Door . . . . . . . . . . . . . . . . . . . . . . . . 20

5  Endless Opportunities . . . . . . . . . . . . . . . . . . 22

6  Supply Is Released . . . . . . . . . . . . . . . . . . . . . 24

7  Perfect Faith . . . . . . . . . . . . . . . . . . . . . . . . . . 26

8  Resentment Be Gone . . . . . . . . . . . . . . . . . . . 28

9  With Love . . . . . . . . . . . . . . . . . . . . . . . . . . . . 30

10  Unless... . . . . . . . . . . . . . . . . . . . . . . . . . . . . . 32

11  A Corrupted Picture . . . . . . . . . . . . . . . . . . . 34

12  Acquitted or Condemned . . . . . . . . . . . . . . . 36

13  Faith Unfurled . . . . . . . . . . . . . . . . . . . . . . . . 38

14  Active Faith . . . . . . . . . . . . . . . . . . . . . . . . . . 40

15  Divine Design . . . . . . . . . . . . . . . . . . . . . . . . . 42

16  Unexpected Wonders . . . . . . . . . . . . . . . . . . 44

17  You Reap What You Sow . . . . . . . . . . . . . . . . 46

18  Imaginations . . . . . . . . . . . . . . . . . . . . . . . . . 48

19  Departments of the Mind . . . . . . . . . . . . . . . 50

20 The Superconscious Mind . . . . . . . . . . . . . . . . . . . 52

21 Idle-Word Disasters . . . . . . . . . . . . . . . . . . . . . . 54

22 From Lack to Plenty . . . . . . . . . . . . . . . . . . . . . . 56

23 Make the First Move . . . . . . . . . . . . . . . . . . . . . . 58

24 Substitute Faith for Fear . . . . . . . . . . . . . . . . . . . 60

25 Ever-Present Listener . . . . . . . . . . . . . . . . . . . . . 62

26 Prepare for Success . . . . . . . . . . . . . . . . . . . . . . 64

27 False Ideas Obliterated . . . . . . . . . . . . . . . . . . . . 66

28 Army of Aliens . . . . . . . . . . . . . . . . . . . . . . . . . 68

29 Goodness and Mercy . . . . . . . . . . . . . . . . . . . . . 70

30 Two Agree . . . . . . . . . . . . . . . . . . . . . . . . . . . . 74

31 Lucky Monkey . . . . . . . . . . . . . . . . . . . . . . . . . . 76

32 God, the Power . . . . . . . . . . . . . . . . . . . . . . . . . 78

33 Superstitions . . . . . . . . . . . . . . . . . . . . . . . . . . 80

34 Hatred Versus Love . . . . . . . . . . . . . . . . . . . . . . 82

35 Courage . . . . . . . . . . . . . . . . . . . . . . . . . . . . . 84

36 Love One Another . . . . . . . . . . . . . . . . . . . . . . . 86

37 Who's the Matter with You? . . . . . . . . . . . . . . . . . 88

38 Your Interests Are Protected . . . . . . . . . . . . . . . . . 90

39 Non-Resistance . . . . . . . . . . . . . . . . . . . . . . . . . 92

40 Picture Perfect . . . . . . . . . . . . . . . . . . . . . . . . . 94

41 One Power, God . . . . . . . . . . . . . . . . . . . . . . . . . 96

42 Bless Your Enemy . . . . . . . . . . . . . . . . . . . . . . . . 98

43 Faults . . . . . . . . . . . . . . . . . . . . . . . . . . . . . . 100

44 Don't Live in the Past . . . . . . . . . . . . . . . . . . . . 102

45 Today Is Completion Day . . . . . . . . . . . . . . . . . 104

46 Boomerangs . . . . . . . . . . . . . . . . . . . . . . . . 108

47 The Lord, the Law . . . . . . . . . . . . . . . . . . . . . .110

48 You Shall Not Covet . . . . . . . . . . . . . . . . . . . . .112

49 Stand Ye Still . . . . . . . . . . . . . . . . . . . . . . .114

50 The Law of Forgiveness . . . . . . . . . . . . . . . . . . .116

51 Order Versus Disorder . . . . . . . . . . . . . . . . . . .118

52 Wise Investments . . . . . . . . . . . . . . . . . . . . . 120

53 According to Your Faith . . . . . . . . . . . . . . . . . . 122

54 Hope Chest . . . . . . . . . . . . . . . . . . . . . . . 124

55 Under Grace . . . . . . . . . . . . . . . . . . . . . . 126

56 Lighten Your Burden . . . . . . . . . . . . . . . . . . 128

57 I Go Free . . . . . . . . . . . . . . . . . . . . . . . . 130

58 The Manifestation of Good . . . . . . . . . . . . . . . 132

59 Believe . . . . . . . . . . . . . . . . . . . . . . . . . 134

60 With Music and Dancing . . . . . . . . . . . . . . . . 136

61 Choose Whom You Will Serve . . . . . . . . . . . . . 138

62 Vain Imaginations . . . . . . . . . . . . . . . . . . . . 140

63 Real Love . . . . . . . . . . . . . . . . . . . . . . . . 142

64 Love Your Work . . . . . . . . . . . . . . . . . . . . . 144

65 No Hoarding Allowed . . . . . . . . . . . . . . . . . . 146

66 Self-Destruction Versus Love . . . . . . . . . . . . . . 148

67 Fear Not . . . . . . . . . . . . . . . . . . . . . . . . . 150

68 Ask and Receive . . . . . . . . . . . . . . . . . . . . . 152

69 Giving and Receiving. . . . . . . . . . . . . . . . . . . 154

70 Intuition . . . . . . . . . . . . . . . . . . . . . . . . . . 156

71 Congestion . . . . . . . . . . . . . . . . . . . . . . . . 158

72 Permanent Healing. . . . . . . . . . . . . . . . . . . . 160

73 Indecision, a Stumbling Block . . . . . . . . . . . . . 162

74 Lost and Found . . . . . . . . . . . . . . . . . . . . . 164

75 No Debt. . . . . . . . . . . . . . . . . . . . . . . . . . 166

76 Mountain-Moving Faith . . . . . . . . . . . . . . . . . 168

77 An Effort of the Will. . . . . . . . . . . . . . . . . . . 170

78 Will It Ever Clear Up? . . . . . . . . . . . . . . . . . . 172

79 Surprises! . . . . . . . . . . . . . . . . . . . . . . . . . 174

80 Pour Out a Blessing. . . . . . . . . . . . . . . . . . . 178

81 Perfect Divine Design. . . . . . . . . . . . . . . . . . 180

82 The Science of the Mind . . . . . . . . . . . . . . . . 182

83 In All Your Ways . . . . . . . . . . . . . . . . . . . . . 184

84 A Supply for Every Demand . . . . . . . . . . . . . . 186

85 A Matter of Consciousness. . . . . . . . . . . . . . . 188

86 Rejoice! . . . . . . . . . . . . . . . . . . . . . . . . . . 190

87 Subconscious Power . . . . . . . . . . . . . . . . . . 192

88 Decreed and Manifested. . . . . . . . . . . . . . . . 194

89 Cheerful Receivers . . . . . . . . . . . . . . . . . . . 196

90 Your Request Is Granted . . . . . . . . . . . . . . . . 198

About Florence Scovel Shinn. . . . . . . . . . . . . . 201

# BONUS GIFT

Get your free ebook and try out our newsletter here:

www.soundwisdom.com/classics

## THANK YOU FOR
## PURCHASING THIS BOOK!

# Foreword

Each of the *90 Daily Decrees and Affirmations for Prosperity* are thought-provoking and mega-motivating. Author Florence Scovel Shinn's writings are unique and include her personal "positive thought" philosophy, supported by her many students' experiences, with whom she shared instructions, treatments, and affirmations.

Shinn's perspective on self-consciousness and how people have more control over their circumstances than they realize established her as a well-known "New Thought" author in the early 19th century.

She references the Bible, real-life experiences, and explores metaphysics—the nature and origin of reality itself, the immortal soul, and the existence of a Supreme Being. The result is an enjoyable, informative, and exciting recipe for success in every area of life.

From financial, vocational, spiritual, social, relational, mental, emotional, and physical to all other aspects of living, these taken-seriously decrees and affirmations will bring prosperity and harmony into your daily living. Creating a prosperous life-style is not only doable, it is as easy as believing, repeating, and receiving.

You will read about true-life miracles of provision, healing, restoration, forgiveness, and much more—all benefits and gains that will not only enhance you personally and professionally but will also take all your relationships to a new level of satisfaction and peace.

You will also read about how *not* to attract: financial ruin; fear and doubt and worry; family disasters; promotion setbacks; negative circumstances; ill health, etc.

We believe that you will reap exactly what you sow—a fruitful and prosperous harvest—after reading this encouraging and most interesting compilation of teachings, stories, decrees and affirmations.

# 1

# The Word's Power

We know that words and thoughts are a tremendous vibratory force, ever-molding our body and affairs. God said through Isaiah, "So shall My word be that goes forth from My mouth; it shall not return to Me void, but it shall accomplish what I please, and it shall prosper in the thing for which I sent it" (Isaiah 55:11 NKJV).

A woman came to me in great distress and said she was to be sued on the 15th of the month for $3,000. She knew no way of getting the money and was in despair. I told her that God was her supply and that there is a supply for every demand, so I spoke the word. I gave thanks that the woman would receive $3,000 at the right time in the right way. I told her she must have perfect faith and act on her perfect faith.

The 15th came, but no money had materialized. She called me and asked what she was to do. I replied, "It is Saturday, so they won't sue you today. Your part is to act rich, thereby showing perfect faith that you will receive it by Monday." She asked me to lunch with her to keep up her courage. When I joined her at a restaurant, I said, "This is no time to economize. Order an expensive luncheon and act as if you have already received the $3,000. All things, whatsoever ye ask in prayer, believing, ye shall receive. You must act as if you had already received." The next morning, she called me and asked me to stay with her during the day. I said "No, you are divinely protected, and God is never too late."

In the evening, she phoned again, greatly excited and said, "My dear, a miracle has happened. I was sitting in my room this morning when the doorbell rang. I said to the maid, 'Don't let anyone in.' The maid, however, looked out the window and said, 'It's your cousin with the long white beard.'

So I said, 'Call him back. I would like to see him.' He was just turning the corner when he heard the maid's voice, and he came back. He talked for about an hour, and just as he was leaving he said, 'Oh, by the way, how are finances?' I told him I needed the money, and he said, 'Why, my dear, I will give you $3,000 the first of the month.' I didn't like to tell him I was going to be sued. What shall I do? I won't receive it till the first of the month, and I must have it tomorrow."

I said, "The Infinite Spirit is never too late. I give thanks she has received the money and that it manifests on time." The next morning her cousin called her up and said, "Come to my office this morning, and I will give you the money." That afternoon, she had $3,000 to her credit in the bank and wrote checks as rapidly as her excitement would permit.

14

# DECREE

## AND

# AFFIRMATION

*God's powerful word will be accomplished in my life.*

*I will study and stand firm on God's Word.*

# 2

# The Power of Your Words

We have the power to change an unhappy condition by waving God's word, which brings abundance. In the place of sorrow appears joy, in the place of sickness appears health, in the place of lack appears plenty.

For example, a woman came for a treatment for prosperity. She possessed just $2 in the world. I said, "We bless the $2 and know that you have the "purse of the spirit." It can never be depleted. As money goes out, immediately, money comes in under grace and imperfect ways. I see it always crammed, jammed with money. Green bills, pink checks, blue checks, white checks, gold, silver, and all kinds of currency. I see it bulging with abundance."

She replied, "I feel my bag heavy with money," and was so filled with faith that she gave me one of her dollars as a love offering. I did not dare refuse it and see lack for her, as it was important that I hold the picture of her plenty.

Shortly afterward, she was made a gift of $6,000. Fearless faith and the spoken word brought it to pass.

The affirmation of a full purse is very powerful, as it brings a vivid picture to the mind. It is impossible not to see your purse or wallet filled with money when using the words "crammed, jammed."

The human imaging faculty is creative, and it is important to choose words that bring a flash of the fulfillment of the demand. Never force a picture by visualizing. Let the divine idea flash into your conscious mind. Then you are working according to the divine design.

# DECREE

## AND

# AFFIRMATION

*I declare that all my needs are met, in Jesus's name.*

*I affirm that my bank accounts are overflowing with deposits.*

# 3

# Truth Sets You Free

"Then you will know the truth, and the truth will set you free." This Scripture verse means that we must know the truth of every situation that confronts us. *There is no truth in lack or limitation.* God waves over His word and the wilderness rejoices and blossoms as the rose.

Fear, doubt, anxiety, anger, and resentment pull down the cells of the body, shock the nervous system, and are the causes of disease and disaster. Happiness and health must be earned by absolute control of the emotional nature.

Power moves but is never moved. When we stand calm and serene, have a good appetite, feel content and happy when appearances are against us, we have reached mastery in life. Then we have the power to rebuke the winds and the waves to control conditions. God's Word and our words transmute *apparent failure into success*—and we know His universal supply is endless and immediate and all our needs manifest instantly on the external.

For example, a woman at sea awoke in the morning hearing the fog horns blowing. A dense fog had settled on the ocean with no apparent signs of clearing. She immediately spoke the word, "There are no fogs in His divine mind, so let the fog be lifted. *I give thanks for the sun.*"

Soon the sun came out, for humans have dominion over the elements, over all created things. Every person has power to lift the fog in our life. It may be a fog of lack of money, love, happiness, or health. Give thanks for the sun.

# DECREE

## AND

# AFFIRMATION

*I decree that there is no truth in lack or limitation—I stand on God's truth of plenty.*

*I affirm my dominion over every fog and give thanks for the Son!*

# 4

# An Open Door

There are certain words or pictures which impress the subconscious mind. For example, a man came asking me to speak the word for his right work, a job. I gave him the statement, *"Behold, I have set before thee the open door of destiny and no man shall shut it."*

It didn't seem to make much of an impression with him, so I was inspired to add, "And no man shall shut it for it is nailed back."

The man was electrified and went out walking on air. Within a few weeks, he was called to a distant city to fill a wonderful position, which came about in a miraculous way.

I give another example of a woman who fearlessly followed a hunch. She was working for a small salary when she read my book, *The Game of Life and How to Play It.* The thought came in a flash to start in business for herself and open a tea room and candy shop.

The idea staggered her at first, but it persisted so she boldly went forth and procured a shop and assistants. She spoke the word for supply, for she did not have money to back her enterprise. The resources came in miraculous ways, and then the shop opened. From the first day, it was filled with people and now it is crammed, jammed. They stand in line and wait.

One day being a holiday, her assistants became gloomy and said they did not expect to do much business. My student, however, replied that *God was her supply and every day was a good day.* In the afternoon, an old friend came in to see the shop and bought two pounds of candy. He gave her a check and when she looked at it, she found it was for $100, so it was indeed a good day. One hundred dollars for a box of candy. She says every morning she enters the shop with wonder and *gives thanks that she had the fearless faith that wins.*

# DECREE

## AND

# AFFIRMATION

*I decree that God is my supply and every day is a good day.*

*I affirm that I have fearless faith that wins!*

# 5

# Endless Opportunities

*uccess affirmations:* I clap my cymbals and rejoice for Jehovah goes before me making clear, easy and successful my way. I give thanks for my whirlwind success. I sweep all before me for I work with His Spirit and follow the divine plan of my life. My spiritual sporting blood is up. I am more than equal to this situation. I am awake to my good and gather in the harvest of endless opportunities. I am harmonious, poised and magnetic.

*Declarations:* I now draw to myself my own. My power is God's power and is irresistible. Divine order is now established in my mind, body and affairs. I see clearly and act quickly, and my greatest expectations come to pass in a miraculous way. There is no competition on this spiritual plane.

*Future foundations:* I have within me an undiscovered country that is revealed to me now in the name of Jesus Christ. Behold, I have set before the open door of destiny and no one shall shut it, for it is nailed back. The tide of destiny has turned and everything comes my way. I banish the past and now live in the wonderful now, where happy surprises come to me each day. There are no lost opportunities in divine mind. As one door shuts, another door opens. The genius within me is now released. I now fulfill my destiny.

# DECREE
## AND
# AFFIRMATION

*I decree that what is rightfully mine is given to me under grace.*

*I affirm that the Christ in me is risen.*

# 6

# Supply Is Released

We come into the world financed by God with all that He desires or requires already on our pathway. This supply is released through faith and the spoken word. If you can believe, all things are possible.

For example, a woman came to me one day to tell me of her experience in using an affirmation she had read in my book. She was without experience but desired a good position on the stage. She spoke the affirmation consistently, "Infinite Spirit, open the way for my great abundance. I am an irresistible magnet for all things that belong to me by divine right."

She was given a very important part in a successful opera. She said, "It was a miracle due to that affirmation which I repeated hundreds of times."

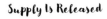

# DECREE

## AND

# AFFIRMATION

*I decree that I'm awake to my good and gather
in the harvest of endless opportunities.*

*I affirm that, I am harmonious, poised and magnetic.*

# 7

# Perfect Faith

In that wonderful moving picture, *The Thief of Baghdad*, we were told in letters of light that happiness must be earned. I believe it is earned through perfect control of the emotional nature. There can be no happiness where there is fear, apprehension, or dread. With perfect faith in God comes a feeling of security and happiness.

When we know that there is an invincible power who protects us and all that we love and brings to us every righteous desire of the heart, we relax all nervous tension and are happy and satisfied. We can be undisturbed by adverse appearances, knowing that God is protecting His interest and utilizing every situation to bring His good to pass.

# DECREE

## AND

# AFFIRMATION

*I decree that there are no lost opportunities in the Kingdom. As one door shuts, another door opens. There is nothing to fear, for there is no power to hurt.*

*I affirm walking up to the lion on my pathway and find an angel in armor and victory in the name of Jesus Christ.*

# 8

# Resentment Be Gone

esentment has ruined more homes than drunkenness and killed more people than war. For example, there was a woman who was healthy and happy and married to a man she loved. The man died and left part of his estate to a relative. The woman was filled with resentment. She lost weight, was unable to do her work, developed gallstones, and became very ill.

A metaphysician called upon her one day. He said, "Woman, see what hate and resentment have done to you? They have caused hard stones to form in your body and only forgiveness and goodwill can cure you."

The woman saw the truth of this statement. She became harmonious and forgiving and regained her splendid health.

*Surely resentment destroys the fool, and jealousy kills the simple* (**Job 5:2 NLT**).

# DECREE

## AND

# AFFIRMATION

*I decree that I am in perfect harmony. I stand aside and let God make easy and successful my way.*

*I affirm that new fields of divine activity now open for me. Unexpected doors fly open for me.*

# 9

# With Love

With love can come terrific fear. Nearly every human comes into the world with a mythical rival in the back of his or her mind who is there to rob him or her of love.

For instance, she has been called the "other woman." Of course it comes from a person's belief and duality. So long as a woman visualizes interference, it will come. The same is true for a man.

It is usually very difficult for a woman to see herself loved by the man she loves. It is often very difficult as well for a man to see himself loved by the woman he loves. So these affirmations are to impress the truth of the situation upon one's subconscious mind, for in reality there is only oneness.

# DECREE

## AND

# AFFIRMATION

*I decree that what God has done for others He can do for me and more. I am as necessary to God as He is to me, for I am the channel to bring His plan to pass.*

*I affirm that I will not limit God by seeing limitation in myself. With God and myself, all things are possible.*

# Unless...

Unless marriage is built upon the rock of oneness, it cannot stand. Two souls with but a single thought, two hearts that beat as one. The poet understood this, for unless husband and wife are living the same thoughts, they must inevitably drift apart.

Thought is a tremendous vibratory force and humans are drawn to their thought creations. For example, a man and woman married and were apparently happy. The man became successful and his taste improved, but the wife still lived in a limited consciousness.

Whenever the man bought anything, he went to the best shops and selected what he needed regardless of price. Whenever the wife went out, she haunted the 5 and 10 cent stores. He was living, in thought, on Fifth Avenue, and her thought world was on Third Avenue. Eventually, the break and separation came.

There is for each person his or her other half or divine selection. These two are one in their thought worlds. These are the two whom God has joined together and no one shall or can part asunder. The twain shall be made one, for in the superconscious mind of each is the same divine plan.

# DECREE

## AND

# AFFIRMATION

*I decree that giving precedes receiving and my gifts to others precede God's gifts to me. Every person is a golden link in the chain of my good.*

*I affirm that my poise is built upon a rock. I see clearly and act quickly. God cannot fail, so I cannot fail.*

# A Corrupted Picture

Whatever you dislike or hate will surely come upon you; for when we hate, we make a vivid yet corrupted picture in the subconscious mind and it objectifies. The only way to erase these pictures is through non-resistance.

For example, a woman was interested in a man who told her repeatedly of his charming female cousins. She was jealous and resentful and he passed out of her life.

Later on, she met another man to whom she was much attracted. In the course of their conversation, he mentioned some women, cousins he was very fond of. She resented it and then laughed, for here were her old "friends," the cousins, back again.

This time she tried non-resistance. She blessed all the cousins in the universe and sent them goodwill for she knew if she didn't, every man she met would be stocked up with women relations. This solution was successful, for she never heard cousins mentioned again.

# DECREE

## AND

# AFFIRMATION

*I decree that the warrior within me has already won.*

*I affirm that God's Kingdom is within me and that His will be done in me and my affairs.*

35

## 12

# Acquitted or Condemned

Many people have unhappy experiences repeated in their lives. For instance, I knew a woman who bragged of her troubles. She would go about saying to people, "I know what trouble is," and then waited for their words of sympathy.

Of course, the more she mentioned her troubles, the more she had; for by her words, she was condemned. She should have used her words to neutralize her troubles instead of multiply them.

For example, if she would have said repeatedly, "I cast every burden upon the Christ within and I go free," and did not voice her sorrows, they would have faded from her life—for by your words, you are justified.

# DECREE

## AND

# AFFIRMATION

*I decree that I make friends with hindrances
and every obstacle becomes a stepping stone.*

*I affirm that everything in the universe, visible
and invisible, is working to bring me to my own.*

# 13

# Faith Unfurled

Humans are ever-reaping on the external what they have sown in their thought world. For example, a woman needed money and was walking along the street making the affirmation that God was her immediate supply.

She looked down at her feet and there was a $2 bill, which she picked up. A man standing near, a watchman in a building, said to her, "Lady, did you pick up some money? I thought it was a piece of chewing gum paper. A lot of people walked over it, but when you came, it opened up like a leaf."

The others, thinking lack, had passed over it, but at her words of faith, it unfurled. So it is with the opportunities in life. One person sees, another passes by. Faith without works or action is dead.

# DECREE

## AND

# AFFIRMATION

*I decree thanks that the walls of Jericho fall down
and all lack, limitation and failure are wiped out
of my consciousness in the name of Jesus Christ.*

*I affirm that I am now on the royal road
of success, happiness, and abundance.
All the traffic goes my way.*

# 14

# Active Faith

To bring into manifestation the answer to your prayer, you must show active faith. For example, a woman came to me asking me to speak the word for the renting a room in her home. I gave her the statement, "I give thanks that the room is now rented to the right and perfect person for the right price, giving perfect satisfaction."

Several weeks elapsed, but the room had not been rented. I asked, "Have you shown active faith? Have you followed every hunch in regard to the room?"

She replied, "I had a hunch to get a lamp for the room, but I decided I couldn't afford it."

I said, "You'll never rent the room until you get that lamp, for in buying the lamp, you are acting on your faith, impressing the subconscious mind with certainty. What is the price of the lamp?"

"Four dollars."

I exclaimed, "Four dollars is standing between you and the perfect renter!"

She became so enthusiastic, she bought two lamps. About a week elapsed and in walked the perfect renter. He did not smoke and paid the rent in advance and fulfilled her ideal in every way.

# DECREE

## AND

# AFFIRMATION

*I decree that I will not weary of well-doing
for when I least expect it, I shall reap.*

*I affirm that Jehovah goes before me and the battle
is won. All enemy thoughts are wiped out.*

# 15

# Divine Design

Without vision, people perish. Unless we have some objective, some promised land to look forward to, we begin to perish. We see it so often in small country towns in the men who sit around a stove all winter and have no ambition. Within each one is an undiscovered country, a gold mine.

I knew a man in a country town called Magnolia Charlie because he always found the first magnolia bloom each spring. He was a shoemaker, but every afternoon, left his work to go to the station to meet the 4:15 train from a distant city.

They were the only romances in his life—the first magnolia and the 4:15 train. He felt vaguely the call of the vision in his superconscious mind. No doubt the divine design for him included travel and perhaps he was to become a genius in the plant world.

Through the spoken word, the divine design may be released and each one fulfill his or her destiny. I now see clearly the perfect plan of my life. Divine enthusiasm fires me and I now fulfill my destiny. The spiritual attitude toward money is to know that God is our supply and that we draw from it the abundance of the spheres through our faith and spoken word.

When we realize this, we lose all greed for money and are fearless in letting it go out. With divine design in our spirit, our supply of everything we need is endless and immediate. We also realize that giving precedes receiving.

# DECREE

## AND

# AFFIRMATION

*I decree that I'm victorious in
the name of Jesus Christ.*

*I affirm that there are no obstacles in the divine
mind. Therefore, there is nothing to obstruct my good.*

# Unexpected Wonders

One day a woman came to me asking me to speak the word for $500 by August 1. It was then about July 1. I knew her very well and said, "The trouble with you is you don't give enough. You must open your channels of supply by giving."

She had accepted an invitation to visit a friend and did not want to go because of the formality. She said, "Please speak the word for me to be polite for three weeks and I want to get away as soon as possible and be sure to speak the word for the $500."

So she went to the friend's house, was unhappy and restless and tried continually to leave, but was always persuaded to stay longer. She remembered my advice, however, and gave the people her polite presence. Whenever possible, she made a little gift.

It was nearing the first of August and no signs of the $500 and no way of escape from the visit. The last day of July she said, "Oh God, maybe I haven't given enough," so she tipped all the servants more than she had intended.

August 1 came and her hostess said to her, "My dear, I want to give you a gift," and handed her a check for $500. God works in unexpected ways, His wonders to perform.

# DECREE

## AND

# AFFIRMATION

*I decree that all obstacles now
vanish from my pathway.*

*I affirm that doors fly open, gates are lifted and I
enter the Kingdom of fulfillment under grace.*

## 17

# You Reap What You Sow

Most people consider life a battle, but it is not a battle, it is a game. It is a game, however, that cannot be played successfully without the knowledge of Spiritual Law; and the Old and the New Testaments give the rules of the game with wonderful clearness.

Jesus Christ taught that it was a great game of giving and receiving: whatever we sow is what we will reap. This means that whatever we send out in word or deed will return just the same to us. What we give, we will receive. If we give hate, we will receive hate. If we give love, we will receive love. If we give criticism, we will receive criticism. If we lie, we will be lied to. If we cheats, we will be cheated.

> *Don't be misled—you cannot mock the justice of God. You will always harvest what you plant* (**Galatians 6:7 NLT**).

# DECREE

## AND

# AFFIRMATION

*I decree rhythm, harmony and balance are now
established in my mind, body and affairs.*

*I affirm that new fields of divine activity now open
for me and these fields are white with the harvest.*

# Imaginations

We are taught that the imaging faculty of our minds plays a leading part in life. *"Keep your heart* [or imagination] *with all diligence, for out of it spring the issues of life,"* (Proverbs 4:23 NKJV). This means that what we imagine will sooner or later externalize in our day-to-day experiences.

I know of a man who feared a certain disease. It was a very rare disease and difficult to get, but he pictured it continually and read about it until it manifested in his body, and he died, the victim of a distorted imagination. So to successfully maneuver life, we must train the imaging faculty.

People trained to imagine only good brings into their lives every righteous desire of their heart: health, wealth, love, friends, perfect self-expression, their highest ideals. The imagination has been called the "scissors of the mind," and it is ever-cutting, cutting, day by day, the pictures we sees there—and sooner or later, we meet our own creations in our outer world. To train the imagination successfully, we must understand the workings of our mind. The Greek said, "Know thyself."

# DECREE
## AND
# AFFIRMATION

*I decree that my will is powerless to interfere with God's will. God's will is now done in my mind, body, and affairs.*

*I affirm that God's plan for me is permanent and cannot be budged.*

# 19

# Departments of the Mind

There are three departments of the mind: the subconscious, conscious, and superconscious. The subconscious is simply power without direction. It is like steam or electricity, and it does what it is directed to. It has no power of induction.

Whatever we feel deeply or imagine clearly is impressed upon the subconscious mind and carried out in minutest detail. For example, a woman I know, when a child, always made believe she was a widow. She dressed up in black clothes and wore a long, black veil, and people thought she was very clever and amusing. She grew up and married a man with whom she was deeply in love. In a short time, he died, and she wore black and a sweeping veil for many years.

The picture of herself as a widow was so impressed upon her subconscious mind that in due time it worked itself out regardless of the havoc created. The conscious mind has been called our mortal or carnal mind. It is the human mind and sees life as it appears to be. It sees death, disaster, sickness, poverty, and limitation of every kind, and it impresses the subconscious.

# DECREE

## AND

# AFFIRMATION

*I decree that am true to my heavenly vision.*

*I affirm that the divine plan of my life now takes shape in definite concrete experiences leading to my heart's desire.*

## 20

# The Superconscious Mind

The *superconscious* mind is the God-mind within each human being and is the realm of perfect ideas. In it is the perfect pattern spoken of by Plato, the divine design, for there is a divine design for each person. There is a place that you are to fill and no one else can fill, something you are to do which no one else can do. There is a perfect picture of this in the superconscious mind. It usually flashes across the conscious as an unattainable ideal, something too good to be true.

In reality, it is our true destiny, or destination, flashed to us from the Infinite Intelligence, which is within us. Many people, however, are ignorant of their true destinies and are striving for things in situations that do not belong to them and would only bring failure and dissatisfaction if attained.

For example, a woman came and asked me to speak the word that she would marry a certain man with whom she was very much in love. She called him A.B. I replied that this would be a violation of Spiritual Law, but that I would speak the word for the right man, the divine selection, the man who belongs to her by divine right. I added, "If A.B. is the right man, you can't lose him, and if he isn't, you will receive his equivalent."

She saw A.B. frequently, but no headway was made in their friendship. One evening she called and said, "Do you know, for the last week, A.B. hasn't seemed so wonderful to me." I replied, "Maybe he's not the divine selection. Another man may be the right one." Soon after that, she met another man who fell in love with her at once and who said she was his ideal. In fact, he said all the things that she had always wished A.B. would say to her. She remarked, "It was quite uncanny." She soon returned his love and lost all interest in A.B.

# DECREE

## AND

# AFFIRMATION

*I decree that I now draw from the universal substance with irresistible power and determination that which is mine by divine right.*

*I affirm that I will not resist this situation.*

# 21

# Idle-Word Disasters

Many people have brought disaster into their lives through idle words. For example, a woman once asked me why her life was now one of poverty of limitation. Formerly, she had a home, was surrounded by beautiful things, and had plenty of money. We found she had often tired of the management of her home and had said repeatedly, "I'm sick and tired of things. I wish I lived in a trunk," and she added, "Today I am living in that trunk." She had spoken herself into a trunk.

The subconscious mind has no sense of humor and people often joke themselves into unhappy experiences. For example, a woman who had a great deal of money joked continually about getting ready for the poorhouse. In a few years, she was almost destitute, having impressed the subconscious mind with a picture of lack and limitation.

# DECREE

## AND

# AFFIRMATION

*I confirm that God's divine idea for
my good will now come to pass.*

*I affirm that my good now flows to me in a
steady, unbroken, ever-increasing stream
of success, happiness, and abundance.*

# 22

# From Lack to Plenty

Fortunately, spiritual law works both ways, and a situation of lack may be changed to one of plenty. For example, a woman came to me one hot summer's day for a treatment for prosperity. She was worn out, dejected, and discouraged. She said she possessed just eight dollars in the world. I said, "Good. We'll bless the eight dollars and multiply them as Jesus Christ multiplied the loaves and fishes, for He taught that everyone had the power to bless and to multiply, to heal and to prosper."

She said, "What shall I do next?"

"Follow intuition. Have you a hunch to do anything or to go anywhere?" Intuition means, intuition, or to be taught from within. It is our unerring guide.

The woman replied "I don't know. I seem to have a hunch to go home. I've just enough money for carfare." Her home was in a distant city and was one of lack and limitation, and the reasoning mind, or intellect, would have said, "Stay in New York and get work and make some money."

I replied, "Then go home. Never violate a hunch." I spoke the following words for her: "Infinite Spirit, open the way for great abundance for... She is an irresistible magnet for all that belongs to her by divine right." I told her to repeat it continually. She left for home immediately.

When visiting a woman one day, she linked up with an old friend of her family. Through this friend, she received thousands of dollars in a most miraculous way. She has said to me often, "Tell people about the woman who came to you with eight dollars and a hunch."

There is always plenty on our pathway, but it can only be brought into manifestation through desire, faith, or the spoken word.

# DECREE

## AND

# AFFIRMATION

*I decree that the decks are now cleared for divine action and my own comes to me under grace.*

*I affirm letting go of worn-out conditions and worn-out things.*

# 23

# Make the First Move

J esus Christ brought out clearly that we must make the first move. God is ever ready to carry out our smallest or greatest demands. Every desire, uttered or unexpressed, is a demand. We are often startled by having a wish suddenly fulfilled.

For example, one Easter, having seen many beautiful rose trees in the florists' windows, I wished I would receive one—and for an instant saw it mentally being carried in the door. Easter came, and with it a beautiful rose tree. I thanked my friend the following day and told her it was just what I had wanted. She replied, "I didn't send you a rose tree. I sent you lilies." The man had mixed the order and sent me a rose tree simply because I had started the law in action, and I had to have a rose tree.

Nothing stands between humans and our highest ideals and every desire of our heart—except doubt and fear. When we can wish without worrying, every desire will be instantly fulfilled. Fear must be erased from the consciousness. It is our only enemy: fear of lack, fear of failure, fear of sickness, fear of loss, and a feeling of insecurity on some plane.

# DECREE

## AND

# AFFIRMATION

*I declare that I have fearless faith that produces God's will and my heart's desire.*

*I affirm seeing clearly the blessing God has given me this day.*

# 24

# Substitute Faith for Fear

Jesus Christ said, *"Why are ye fearful, O ye of little faith?"* (Matthew 8:26 KJV). So we can see we must substitute faith for fear, for fear is only inverted faith. It is faith in evil instead of good. The object of life is to see clearly our good and to obliterate all mental pictures of evil. This must be done by impressing the subconscious mind with a realization of good.

A very brilliant man who has attained great success told me he had suddenly erased all fear from his consciousness by reading a sign that hung in a room. He saw printed, in large letters this statement: WHY WORRY? IT WILL PROBABLY NEVER HAPPEN. These words were stamped indelibly upon his subconscious mind, and he has now a firm conviction that only good can come into his life and, therefore, only good can manifest.

# DECREE

## AND

# AFFIRMATION

*I decree that my seeming impossible
good now comes to pass.*

*I affirm that the unexpected now happens.*

## 25

# Ever-Present Listener

The subconscious mind is a faithful servant, but we must be careful to give it the right orders. We have ever a silent listener at our side—our subconscious mind. Every thought, every word is impressed upon it and carried out in amazing detail. It is like a singer making a record on the sensitive disc of the phonographic plate. Every note and tone of the singer's voice is registered. If the singer coughs or hesitates, it is registered also.

So let us break all the old bad records in the subconscious mind, the records of our lives which we do not wish to keep, and make new and beautiful ones. Speak these words aloud with power and conviction: "I now smash and demolish, by my spoken word, every untrue record in my subconscious mind. They shall return to the dust-heap of their native nothingness, for they came from my own vain imaginings. I now make my perfect records through the Christ within, the records of health, wealth, love and perfect self-expression."

# DECREE

## AND

# AFFIRMATION

*I decree that the four winds of success
now blow to me my own.*

*I affirm that from north, south, east
and west comes my endless good.*

# 26

# Prepare for Success

If we ask for success and prepare for failure, we will get the situation we are prepared for. For example, a man came to me asking me to speak the word that a certain debt would be wiped out. I found he spent his time planning what he would say to the man when he did not pay his bill; therefore, neutralizing my words. He should have seen himself paying the debt.

We have a wonderful illustration of this in the Bible, relating to the three kings who were in the desert without water for their men and horses. They consulted the prophet Elisha, who gave them this astonishing message: *"Thus saith the Lord, Make this valley full of ditches. For thus saith the Lord, Ye shall not see wind, neither shall ye see rain; yet that valley shall be filled with water, that ye may drink, both ye, and your cattle, and your beasts"* (2 Kings 3:16-17 KJV).

We must prepare for what we have asked for when there isn't the slightest sign of it in sight.

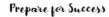

# DECREE

## AND

# AFFIRMATION

*I decree now to draw from the abundance of the spheres my immediate and endless supply.*

*I affirm that all channels are free. All doors are open.*

# 27

# False Ideas Obliterated

To repeat: we must prepare for what we have asked for when there isn't the slightest sign of it in sight. For example, a woman found it necessary to look for an apartment during the year when there was a great shortage of apartments in New York. It was considered almost an impossibility, and her friends were sorry for her and said, "Isn't it too bad? You'll have to store your furniture and live in a hotel."

She replied, "You needn't feel sorry for me. I'm a superman, and I'll get an apartment." She spoke the words, "Infinite Spirit, open the way for the right apartment."

She knew there was a supply for every demand and that she was unconditioned working on the spiritual plane and that one with God is a majority. She had contemplated buying new blankets, when the tempter, the adverse thought or reasoning mind, suggested, "Don't buy the blankets. Perhaps, after all, you won't get an apartment, and you will have no use for them."

She promptly replied to herself, "I'll dig my ditches by buying the blankets." So she prepared for the apartment, acted as though she already had it. She found one in a miraculous way, and it was given to her, although there were more than 200 other applicants. The blankets showed active faith. And it is obvious to say that the ditches dug by the three kings in the desert were filled to overflowing.

# DECREE

## AND

# AFFIRMATION

*I decree that I will prepare for what I have asked for even if there is no sign of it in sight.*

*I affirm that my desert will overflow with life-giving and refreshing water from Heaven.*

# 28

# Army of Aliens

Getting into the spiritual swing of things is no easy matter for the average person. The adverse thoughts of doubt and fear surge from the subconscious. They are the army of aliens, which must be put to flight. This explains why it is so often darkest before the dawn.

A big demonstration is usually preceded by tormenting thoughts. Having made a statement of high spiritual truth, we challenge the old beliefs in the subconscious, and error is exposed to be put out. This is the time when we must make affirmations of truth repeatedly and rejoice and give thanks that we have already received. He will answer before we even ask. This means that every good and perfect gift is already awaiting recognition. We can only receive what we see receiving.

The children of Israel were told that they could have all the land they could see. This is true of us as well. We have only the land within our own mental vision. Every great work, every big accomplishment has been brought into manifestation through holding to the vision, and often just before the big achievement comes apparent failure and discouragement. When the children of God reached the Promised Land, they were afraid to go in because it was filled with giants who made them feel like grasshoppers. This is almost everyone's experience; however, the one who knows Spiritual Law is undisturbed by appearance and rejoices while yet in captivity. That is, we need to hold to our vision and give thanks that the end is accomplished.

# DECREE

## AND

# AFFIRMATION

*I decree that I now release the goldmine within me.*

*I affirm that I'm linked with an endless golden stream of prosperity, which comes to me under grace in perfect ways.*

## 29

# Goodness
# and Mercy

We must ever hold the vision of our journey's end and demand the manifestation of what we have already received. It may be perfect health, love, supply, self-expression, home, or friends. They are all finished and perfect ideas registered in God's divine mind, our own super-conscious mind.

For example, a man came to me asking for treatments for success. It was his imperative that he raise, within a certain time, $50,000 for his business. The time limit was almost up when he came to me in despair. No one wanted to invest in his enterprise, and the bank had flatly refused a loan. I replied, "I suppose you lost your temper while at the bank, therefore, your power. You can control any situation if you first control yourself. Go back to the bank and I will treat."

My treatment for him, "You are identified in love with the spirit of everyone connected with the bank. Let the divine idea come out of this situation."

He replied, "Woman, you are talking about an impossibility. Tomorrow is Saturday. The bank closes at noon, and my train won't get me there until ten, and the time limit is up tomorrow, and anyway, they won't do it. It's too late."

I replied, "God doesn't need any time and is never too late. With Him, all things are possible. I don't know anything about business, but I know all about God."

He replied, "It all sounds fine when I sit here listening to you, but when I go out, it's terrible." He lived in a distant city, and I did not hear from him for a week. Then came a letter. It read, "You were right. I raised the money, and I will never again doubt the truth of all that you told me."

I saw him a few weeks later, and said, "What happened? You evidently had plenty of time after all."

He replied, "My train was late, and I got there 15 minutes till noon. I walked into the bank quietly and said, 'I have come for the loan,' and they gave it to me without a question." It was the last 15 minutes of the time allotted to him—Infinite Spirit was not too late. In this instance the man could never have demonstrated alone. He needed someone to help him hold to the vision. This is what one person can do for another.

# DECREE

## AND

# AFFIRMATION

*I decree and affirm that goodness and mercy shall follow me all the days of my life and I shall dwell in the house of abundance forever.*

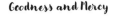
# GOD DOESN'T NEED ANY TIME

### AND

*is never too late.*

# WITH HIM, *all things* ARE POSSIBLE.

# 30

# Two Agree

Jesus Christ knew the truth of helping each other. He said, *"I also tell you this: If two of you agree here on earth concerning anything you ask, my Father in heaven will do it for you"* (Matthew 18:19 NLT). Sometimes we get too close to our own affairs and become doubtful and fearful. The friend, or healer, sees clearly the success, health, or prosperity, and never wavers because he or she is not as close to the situation.

It is much easier to demonstrate for someone else than for oneself, so a person should not hesitate to ask for help if feeling a wavering. A keen observer of life once said, "No man can fail, if some one person sees him successful," such is the power of the vision, and many a great man owed his success to a wife, or sister, or a friend who believed in him and held him without wavering to the perfect pattern.

# DECREE

## AND

# AFFIRMATION

*I decree that my God is the God of plenty and I now receive all that I desire or require and more.*

*I affirm that all that is mine by divine right is now released and reaches me in great avalanches of abundance under grace in miraculous ways.*

# 31

# Lucky Monkey

The horseshoe or rabbit's foot contains no power, but your spoken word and belief that it will bring good fortune creates expectancy in the subconscious mind and attracts a beneficial situation. I find, however, this will not work when we have advanced spiritually and knows a higher law. We cannot turn back, and we must put away graven images.

For example, two men in my class had great success in business for several months, when suddenly everything went to smash. We tried to analyze the situation and I found that instead of making their affirmations and looking to God for success and prosperity, they had each bought a lucky monkey. I said, "Oh I see. You have been trusting in the lucky monkeys instead of God. Put away the lucky monkeys and call on the law of forgiveness, for God will forgive and neutralize your mistakes."

They decided to throw away the lucky monkeys, and all went well again. We must recognize that the only power is God's power who gives to us abundantly.

# DECREE

## AND

# AFFIRMATION

*I decree that my supply is endless,
inexhaustible and immediate and comes
to me under grace in perfect ways.*

*I affirm that all channels are free and open for
my immediate and endless, divinely designed
supply. My ships come on a calm sea.*

# 32

# God, the Power

I was with a friend one day who was in deep despair. In crossing the street, she picked up a horseshoe. Immediately, she was filled with joy and hope. She said God had sent her the horseshoe in order to keep up her courage. It was indeed, at that moment, about the only thing that could have registered in her consciousness. Her hope became faith, and she ultimately made a wonderful demonstration.

I wish to make the point clear that the two men previously mentioned were depending on the monkeys alone, while this woman recognized the Power in back of the horseshoe. I know, in my own case, it took a long while to get out of a belief that a certain thing brought disappointment. If the thing happened, disappointment invariably followed. I found the only way I could make a change in the subconscious was by asserting there are not two powers, *there is only one Power,* God; therefore, there are no disappointments, and this thing means a happy surprise. I noticed a change at once, and happy surprises commenced coming my way.

# DECREE

## AND

# AFFIRMATION

*I decree under direct inspiration, wisely and fearlessly, knowing all my success is endless and immediate and solely comes from God.*

*I affirm that I am fearless in letting idols go, knowing God is my immediate and endless supply.*

# 33

# Superstitions

I have a friend who said nothing could induce her to walk under a ladder. I said, "If you are afraid, you are giving in to a belief in two powers, good and evil, instead of one. As God is absolute, there can be no opposing power unless you make the false of evil for yourself. To show you believe in only one power, God, and that there is no power or reality in evil, walk under the next ladder you see."

Soon after, she went to her bank. She wished to open her box in the safety deposit vault, and there stood a ladder on her pathway. It was impossible to reach the box without passing under the ladder. She quailed with fear and turned back. She could not face the lion on her pathway; however, when she reached the street, my words rang in her ears and she decided to return and walk under it.

It was a big moment in her life, for ladders had held her in bondage for years. She retraced her steps to the vault, and the ladder was no longer there. This so often happens. If you are willing to do something you are afraid to do, you will be set free. It is the law of non-resistance, which is so little understood.

# DECREE

## AND

# AFFIRMATION

*I decree that I will not follow the
desires of my sinful nature.*

*I affirm that I will not be held
captive by superstitions.*

# 34

# Hatred Versus Love

There was a woman who was healthy and happy and married to a man she loved. The man died and left part of his estate to a relative. The woman was filled with resentment. She lost weight, was unable to do her work, developed gallstones and became very ill.

A metaphysician called upon her one day. He said, "Woman, see what hate and resentment have done to you? They have caused hard stones to form in your body and only forgiveness and goodwill can cure you."

The woman saw the truth of this statement. She became harmonious and forgiving and regained her splendid health.

# DECREE

## AND

# AFFIRMATION

*I decree that anger, resentment, ill will, jealousy and revenge rob people of their happiness and bring sickness, failure and poverty in their wake.*

*I affirm that resentment has ruined more homes than drink and killed more people than war.*

# 35

## Courage

Invisible forces are ever-working for those who are always pulling the strings themselves, though they don't know it. Owing to the vibratory power of words, whatever we voice, we begin to attract. People who continually speak of disease invariably attract it. After we know the truth, we cannot be too careful of our words.

For example, I have a friend who often says on the phone, "Do come to see me and have an fine old-fashioned chat." This old-fashioned chat means an hour of about 500 to a thousand destructive words, the principle topics being loss, lack, failure, and sickness.

I reply, "No, thank you. I've had enough old-fashioned chats in my life. They are too expensive, but I will be glad to have a new-fashioned chat and talk about what we want, not what we don't want."

There is an old saying that people only dare to use words for three purposes: to heal, bless, or prosper. Curses, like chickens, come home to roost. If we wish to aid someone to success, we are wishing and aiding ourselves to success. The body may be renewed and transformed through the spoken word and clear vision, and disease be completely wiped out of the consciousness. The metaphysician knows that all disease has a mental component, and in order to heal the body we must first heal the soul. The soul is the subconscious mind, and it must be saved from wrong thinking.

# DECREE

## AND

# AFFIRMATION

*I decree that I'm now deluged with the happiness that was planned for me in the beginning.*

*I affirm that my barns are full, my cup flows over with joy. My endless good now comes to me in endless ways.*

# 36

# Love One Another

It is safe to say that all sickness and unhappiness come from the violation of the law of love. Jesus said that His commandment is that we love one another as He loves us.

For example, a woman I know had, for years, an appearance of a terrible skin disease. The doctors told her it was incurable, and she was in despair. She was on the stage, and she feared she would soon have to give up her profession, and she had no other means of support.

She, however, procured a good engagement, and on the opening night, made a great hit. She received flattering notices from the critics and was joyful and elated. The next day she received a notice of dismissal. A man in the cast had been jealous of her success and had caused her to be sent away.

She felt hatred and resentment taking complete possession of her, and she cried out, "Oh, God. Don't let me hate that man." That night, she worked for hours in the silence. She said, "I soon came into a very deep silence. I seemed to be at peace with myself, with the man, and with the whole world. I continued this for two following nights, and on the third day, I found I was healed completely of the skin disease."

In asking for love and goodwill, she had fulfilled the law; for love is the fulfilling of the law, and the disease, which came from subconscious resentment, was wiped out. Continual criticism produces rheumatism, as critical, inharmonious thoughts cause unnatural deposits in the blood, which settle in the joints. False growths are caused by jealousy, hatred, unforgiveness, fear, etc. I believe that every disease is caused by a mind not at ease.

# DECREE
## AND
# AFFIRMATION

*I decree to having a wonderful joy in a wonderful way, and my wonderful joy has come to stay.*

*I affirm that happy surprises come to me each day as I ask for love for all.*

## 37

# Who's the Matter with You?

I said once in my class, "There is no use asking anyone, 'What's the matter with you?' We might just as well say, 'Who's the matter with you?'" Unforgiveness is the most prolific cause of disease. It will harden arteries or liver, and affect the eye-sight. In its train are endless ills. I called on a woman one day who said she was ill from having eaten a poisoned oyster. I replied, "Oh, no. The oyster was harmless. You poisoned the oyster. Who's the matter with you?"

She answered, "Oh, about nineteen people." She had quarreled with nineteen people and had become so inharmonious that she attracted the wrong oyster.

Any inharmony on the external indicates there is mental inharmony. As the within, so the without. Our only enemies are within ourselves. Personality is one of the last enemies to be overcome, as this planet is taking its initiation in love. It was Christ's message, peace on earth, goodwill toward mankind. The enlightened people, therefore, endeavor to perfect themselves upon our neighbors. Our work is to send out goodwill and blessings to everyone, and the marvelous thing is that when we bless someone, that person has no power to harm us.

# DECREE

## AND

# AFFIRMATION

*I decree to look with wonder at what is before me.*

*I affirm to walk boldly up to the lion on my pathway and find it is a friendly puppy.*

# 38

# Your Interests Are Protected

A man came asking me for treatment for success in business. He was selling machinery, and a rival appeared on the scene with what he proclaimed was a better machine, and my friend feared defeat. I said, "First of all, we must wipe out all fear and know that God protects your interest and that the divine idea must come out of the situation. That is, the right machine will be sold by the right man to the right man," and I added, "Don't hold one critical thought toward that man. Bless him all day, and be willing not to sell your machine if it isn't the divine idea."

So he went to the meeting fearless and nonresistant and blessing the other man. He said the outcome was very remarkable. The other man's machine refused to work; therefore he sold his machine without the slightest difficulty.

Goodwill produces a great aura of protection about the one who sends it, and no weapon that is formed against him shall prosper. In other words, love and goodwill destroy the enemies with yourself; therefore, you have no enemies on the external or the internal. There is peace on earth for those who send good-will to others.

# DECREE

## AND

# AFFIRMATION

*I decree that I am harmonious, happy, radiant, detached from the tyranny of fear.*

*I affirm that my happiness is built upon a rock. It is mine now and for all eternity.*

# 39

# Non-Resistance

Paul tells us in Romans 12:21 (NKJV), *"Do not be overcome by evil, but overcome evil with good."* Nothing on earth can resist an absolutely non-resistant person. The Chinese say that water is the most powerful element because it is perfectly non-resistant. It can wear away a rock and sweep all away in its path. Jesus Christ said, *"Ye have heard that it hath been said, An eye for an eye, and a tooth for a tooth: But I say unto you, That ye resist not evil: but whosoever shall smite thee on thy right cheek, turn to him the other also"* (Romans 12:21 KJV). Jesus knew in reality, there is no evil; therefore, nothing to resist. Evil has come from human vain imagination, or a belief in two powers: good and evil.

There is an old legend that Adam and Eve ate of Maya the Tree of Illusion and saw two powers instead of one power, God. Therefore, evil is a false law humans have made for themselves through psychoma, or soul sleep. Soul sleep means that the human soul has been hypnotized by the race belief of sin, sickness, death, etc., which is carnal or mortal thought, and affairs have out-pictured the illusions.

# DECREE

## AND

# AFFIRMATION

*I decree that my good now flows to me in a steady, unbroken, ever-increasing stream of happiness.*

*I affirm that my happiness is God's affair. Therefore, no one can interfere.*

# 40

# Picture Perfect

The human soul is our subconscious mind and whatever we feel deeply, good or bad, is out-pictured by that faithful servant. Our body and affairs show forth what we have been picturing. The sick person has pictured sickness; the poor person, poverty; the rich person, wealth.

Young people often say, "Why do children attract illness when they are too young even to know what it means?" I answer that children are sensitive and receptive to the thoughts of others around them and often out-picture the fears of their parents. Mothers often, unconsciously, attract illness and disaster to their children by continually holding them in thoughts of fear and watching for symptoms. I heard a metaphysician once say, "If you do not run your subconscious mind yourself, someone else will run it for you."

For example, a friend asked a woman if her little girl had had the measles. She replied promptly, "Not yet," which implied that she was expecting the illness and, therefore, preparing the way for what she did not want for herself and child.

The person centered and established in right thinking, the person who sends out only goodwill to others (young and old), and the person who is without fear cannot be touched or influenced by the negative thoughts of others. In fact, if we are that person, we can receive only good thoughts, as we ourselves send forth only good thoughts. Resistance is hell, for it places us in a state of torment.

# DECREE

## AND

# AFFIRMATION

*I decree that God's ideas for me
are perfect and permanent.*

*I affirm that my heart's desire is a perfect idea in
divine mind, incorruptible and indestructible,
and now comes to pass under grace.*

**41**

# One Power, God

A woman who required money who knew the Spiritual Law of opulence was thrown continually in a business-way with a man who made her feel very poor. He talked lack and limitation, and she commenced to catch his poverty thoughts, so she disliked him and blamed him for her failure. She knew in order to demonstrate her supply, she must first feel that she had received. A feeling of opulence must precede its manifestation.

It dawned upon her one day that she was resisting the situation and seeing two powers instead of One, God, so she blessed the man and baptized the situation. "Success," she affirmed. "As there is only one power, God, this man is here for my good and my prosperity," just what he did not seem to be there for.

Soon after that she met through this man a woman who gave her for a service rendered, several thousand dollars, and the man moved to a distant city and faded harmoniously from her life.

# DECREE

## AND

# AFFIRMATION

*I decree that as I am one with God, I am now one with my heart's desire.*

*I affirm my thanks for my permanent happiness, my permanent health, my permanent wealth, my permanent love.*

# 42

# Bless Your Enemy

B less your enemy, and you rob him of his ammunition. His arrows will be transmuted into blessings." This law is true of nations as well as individuals. Bless a nation, send love and goodwill to every inhabitant, and it is robbed of its power to harm. We can only get the right idea of nonresistance through spiritual understanding. My students have often said, "I don't want to be a doormat." I reply, "When you use nonresistance with wisdom, no one will ever be able to walk over you."

An example: One day I was impatiently awaiting an important telephone call. I resisted every call that came in and made no outgoing calls myself, reasoning that it might interfere with the one I was awaiting. Instead, I should have realized that divine ideas never conflict. The call will come at the right time, leaving it to God to arrange, But I commenced to manage things myself. I made the battle mine, not God's, and remained tense and anxious.

The bell did not ring for about an hour, and I glanced at the phone and found the receiver had been off that length of time, and the phone was disconnected. My anxiety, fear, and belief in interference had brought on a total eclipse of the telephone. Realizing what I had done, I commenced blessing the situation at once. I affirmed, "I cannot lose any call that belongs to me by divine right. I am under grace and not under law."

A friend rushed out to the nearest telephone to notify the company to reconnect. My phone was connected at once, and two minutes later, I received a very important call, and about an hour afterward, the one I had been awaiting.

# DECREE

## AND

# AFFIRMATION

*I decree that I am one with God, the undivided One. I am one with my undivided love and undivided happiness.*

*I affirm that the light of Christ within now wipes out all my fear, doubt, anger and resentment.*

# 43

# Faults

People have said to me, "Give treatments to change my husband or my brother." I reply, "No. I will give treatments to change you. When you change, your husband and your brother will change."

One of my students was in the habit of lying. I told her it was a failure method, and if she lied, she would be lied to. She replied, "I don't care. I can't possibly get along without lying." One day she was speaking on the phone to a man with whom she was very much in love. She turned to me and said, "I don't trust him. I know he's lying to me."

I replied, "Well, you lie yourself, so someone has to lie to you, and you will be sure it will be just the person you want the truth from." Sometime after that, I saw her, and she said, "I'm cured of lying." I questioned, "What cured you?" She replied, "I have been living with a woman who lied worse than I did."

We are often cured of our faults by seeing them in others. Life is a mirror, and we find only ourselves reflected in our associates.

# DECREE

## AND

# AFFIRMATION

*I decree that God's love pours through me
an irresistible, magnetic current.*

*I affirm that I see only perfection
and draw to me my own.*

## 44

# Don't Live in the Past

L iving in the past is a failure method and a violation of Spiritual Law. Lot's wife looked back and was turned into a pillar of salt. The robbers of time are the past and the future. We should bless the past and forget it if it keeps us in bondage—and bless the future knowing it has in store for us, endless joys. But we must live fully in the now.

For example, a woman came to me, complaining that she had no money with which to buy Christmas gifts. She said, "Last year was so different. I had plenty of money and gave lovely presents; and this year, I have scarcely a cent."

I replied, "You will never demonstrate money while you are pathetic and live in the past. Live fully in the now, and get ready to give Christmas presents. Dig your ditches, and the money will come."

She exclaimed, "I know what to do. I'll buy some tinsel, twine, Christmas seals, and wrapping paper."

I replied, "Do that, and the presents will come and stick themselves to the Christmas seals."

This was showing financial fearlessness and faith in God as the reasoning mind said, "Keep every cent you have as you are not sure you will get any more." She bought her seals, paper, and twine, and a few days before Christmas received a gift of several hundred dollars. Buying the seals and twine had impressed the subconscious with expectancy and opened the way for the manifestation of the money. She purchased all the presents in plenty of time.

We must live suspended in the moment. "Look well, therefore, to this day. Such is the salutation of the dawn." We must be spiritually alert, ever-waiting our leads, taking advantage of every opportunity.

# DECREE

## AND

# AFFIRMATION

*I decree divine love through me now dissolves all seeming obstacles and makes clear, easy and successful my way.*

*I affirm living in the now—accepting all the future has for me.*

# 45

# Today Is Completion Day

One day, I said continually, silently, "Infinite Spirit, don't let me miss anything You have for me," and something very important was told to me that evening. It is most necessary to begin the day with right words. Make an affirmation immediately upon waking. For example, "Thy will be done this day. Today is a day of completion. I give thanks for this perfect day. Miracle shall follow miracle, and wonders shall never cease." Make this a habit, and you will see wonders and miracles come into your life.

One morning I picked up a book and read, "Look with wonder at that which is before you." It seemed to be my message for the day, so I repeated again and again, "Look with wonder at that which is before you." At about noon, a large sum of money was given me, which I had been desiring for a certain purpose.

You should never use an affirmation unless it is absolutely satisfying and convincing to your own consciousness, and often, an affirmation is changed to suit different people. For example, the following has brought success to many: "I have a wonderful work in a wonderful way. I give wonderful service for wonderful pay."

I gave the first two lines to one of my students, and she went about singing it aloud and soon did receive wonderful work in a wonderful way and gave wonderful service for wonderful pay. Another student, a business man, took it and changed the word to business. He repeated, "I have a wonderful business in a wonderful way, and I give wonderful service for wonderful pay." That afternoon, he made a $41,000 deal, though there had been no activity in his affairs for months.

Every affirmation must be carefully worded and completely cover the ground. For example, I knew a woman who was in great need and made a demand for work. She received a great deal of work, but was never paid anything. She now knows to add, "Wonderful service for wonderful pay." It is our divine right to have plenty, more than enough. This is God's idea, and when we break down the barriers of lack in our own consciousness, the golden age will be ours and every righteous desire of our heart fulfilled.

# DECREE

## AND

# AFFIRMATION

*I decree that my apparent enemy becomes my friend, a golden link in the chain of my good.*

*I affirm that I'm at peace with myself and with the world.*

IT IS

# MOST

# NECESSARY

TO

## begin the day

WITH

# RIGHT

# WORDS.

# 46

# Boomerangs

We receive only what we give. Life is a game of boomerangs. Our thoughts, deeds, and words return to us sooner or later with astounding accuracy. This is the law of karma, which is Sanskrit for "comeback," or you reap what you sow.

For example, a friend told me this story of herself illustrating the law. She said, "I make all my karma on my aunt. Whatever I say to her, someone says to me. I am often irritable at home, when one day said to my aunt who was talking to me during dinner, 'No more talk. I wish to eat in peace.' The following day, I was lunching with a woman with whom I wished to make a great impression. I was talking animatedly when she said, 'No more talk, I wish to eat in peace.'"

My friend is high in consciousness, so her karma returns much more quickly than to someone merely on the mental plane. The more we know, the more we are responsible for, and a person with a knowledge of Spiritual Law but does not practice it, suffers greatly in consequence.

# DECREE

## AND

# AFFIRMATION

*I decree that I am free from mistakes
and the consequences of mistakes.*

*I affirm that I'm under grace and
not under karmic law.*

# 47

# The Lord, the Law

"*The fear of the Lord* [law] *is the beginning of wisdom.*" If we read the word "Lord" as "law," it will make many passages in the Bible much clearer. "*Vengeance is Mine, and recompense,*" says the Lord in Deuteronomy 32:35 (NKJV). The law takes vengeance, not God. God sees humankind perfect, created in His own image, imagination, and given power and dominion.

This is the perfect idea of a human, registered in God's divine mind, awaiting our recognition, for we can only be what we see ourselves to be and only attain what we see ourselves attaining. "Nothing ever happens without an onlooker" is an ancient saying. We first see our failure or success, our joy or sorrow before it swings into visibility from the scenes set in our own imagination.

# DECREE

## AND

# AFFIRMATION

*I decree that though my mistakes be as scarlet,*
*I shall be washed whiter than snow.*

*I affirm that what didn't happen in the*
*Kingdom never happened anywhere.*

# 48

# You Shall Not Covet

Obedience precedes authority, and the law obeys us when we obey the law. The law of electricity must be obeyed before it becomes our servant. When handled ignorantly, it becomes our deadly foe, so with the laws of mind.

For example, a woman with a strong personal will wished she owned a house that belonged to an acquaintance, and she often made mental pictures of herself living in the house. In the course of time, the man died, and she moved into the house. Several years afterward, coming into the knowledge of Spiritual Law, she said to me, "Do you think I had anything to do with that man's death?"

I replied, "Yes. Your desire was so strong, everything made way for it, but you paid your karmic debt. Your husband, whom you loved devotedly, died soon after, and the house was a white elephant on your hands for many years."

The original owner, however, could not have been affected by her thoughts had he been positive in the truth, nor her husband, but they were both under karmic law. The woman should have said, feeling the great desire for the house, "Infinite Intelligence, give me the right house, equally as charming as this, the house that is mine by divine right." The divine selection would've given perfect satisfaction and brought good to all. The divine pattern is the only safe pattern to work by.

Desire is a tremendous force and must be directed in the right channels, or chaos ensues.

In demonstrating, the most important step is the first step, to ask aright. We should always demand only what is ours by divine right. To go back to the illustration, if the woman had taken this attitude, "If this house I desire is mine, I cannot lose it. If it is not, give me its equivalent," then the man might have decided to move out harmoniously, had it been the divine selection for her, or another house would have been substituted. Anything forced into manifestation through personal will is always ill-got and has ever-bad success.

# DECREE

## AND

# AFFIRMATION

*I decree that no good thing will be withheld from whoever walks uprightly.*

*I affirm that there is no power in evil. It is nothing, therefore can only come to nothing.*

# 49

# Stand Ye Still

Believers always get just what we desire when we relinquish all personal will, thereby enabling Infinite Intelligence to work through us. This is the "Stand ye still and see the salvation of the Lord" law.

For example, a woman came to me in great distress. Her daughter had determined to take a very hazardous trip, and the mother was filled with fear. She said she had used every argument, had pointed out the dangers to be encountered, had forbidden her to go, but the daughter became more and more rebellious and determined. I said to the mother, "You are forcing your personal will upon your daughter, which you have no right to do, and your fear of the trip is only attracting it, for we attract what we fear."

I added, "Let go, and take your mental hands off. Put it in God's hands, and use this statement: I put this situation in the hands of Infinite Love and Wisdom. If this trip is the divine plan, I bless it and no longer resist; but if it is not divinely planned, I give thanks that it is now dissolved and dissipated." A day or two after that, her daughter said to her, "Mother, I have given up going on the trip," and the situation returned to its native nothingness.

Learning to stand still, seems so difficult for humans.

# DECREE

## AND

# AFFIRMATION

*I decree that fear and impatience demagnetize. Poise magnetizes.*

*I affirm that I will drown the reasoning mind with my affirmation.*

# 50

# The Law of Forgiveness

nother example of sowing and reaping came in the most curious way. A woman came to me saying she had received a counterfeit $20 bill given to her at the bank. She was much disturbed, for, she said, "The people at the bank will never acknowledge their mistake."

I replied, "Let us analyze the situation and find out why you attracted it."

She thought a few moments and exclaimed, "I know it! I sent a friend a lot of stage money just for a joke."

The law had sent her some stage money, for it doesn't know anything about jokes. I said, "Now we will call on the law of forgiveness and neutralize the situation."

Christianity is founded upon the law of forgiveness. Christ has redeemed us from the curse of the karmic law, and the Christ within each of us is our Redeemer and salvation from all inharmonious conditions, so I said, "Infinite Spirit, we call on the law of forgiveness and give thanks that that woman is under grace and not under law and cannot lose this $20, which is hers by divine right."

"Now," I said, "Go back to the bank and tell them, fearlessly, that it was given you there by mistake." She obeyed and, to her surprise, they apologized and gave her another bill, treating her most courteously. So knowledge of the law gives us power to rub out mistakes.

# DECREE

## AND

# AFFIRMATION

*I decree that I forgive everyone and everyone forgives me.*

*I affirm and call on the law of forgiveness.*

# 51

# Order Versus Disorder

One day a woman came to me asking treatment for prosperity. She did not take much interest in her household affairs, and her home was in great disorder. I said to her, "If you wish to be rich, you much be orderly. All with great wealth are orderly, and order is Heaven's first law." I added, "You will never become rich with a burnt match in the pincushion."

She had a good sense of humor and commenced immediately, putting her house in order. She rearranged furniture, straightened out bureau drawers, cleaned rugs, and soon received a big financial demonstration: a gift from a relative. The woman herself became tidy looking and keeps herself keyed up financially by being ever-watchful of the external and expecting prosperity, knowing God is her supply.

Many people are in ignorance of the fact that gifts and things are investments and that hoarding and saving invariably lead to loss: *"Give freely and become more wealthy; be stingy and lose everything"* (Proverbs 11:24 NLT).

# DECREE

## AND

# AFFIRMATION

*I decree that there is always a
way out of every solution.*

*I affirm that under grace, everyone
is free to do the will of God.*

# 52

# Wise Investments

I knew a man who wanted to buy a fur-lined overcoat. He and his wife went to various shops, but there was none he wanted. He said they were all too cheap looking. At last, he was shown one the salesman said was valued at $1,000 but which the manager would sell him for $500 as it was late in the season. His financial possessions amounted to about $700.

The reasoning mind would have said, "You can't afford to spend nearly all you have on a coat," but he was very intuitive and never reasoned. He turned to his wife and said, "If I get this coat, I'll make a ton of money," so his wife consented, weakly. About a month later, he received a $10,000 commission. The coat made him feel so rich, it linked him with success and prosperity. Without the coat, he would not have received the commission. It was an investment paying large dividends.

If we ignore these leadings to spend or to give, the same amount of money will go in an uninteresting or unhappy way.

# DECREE

## AND

# AFFIRMATION

*I decree that sureism is stronger than optimism.*

*I affirm that divine ideas never conflict.*

# 53

# According to Your Faith

Another example of when we ignore leadings to spend or to give, is of a woman who told me that she informed her family that they could not afford a Thanksgiving dinner. She had the money, but decided to save it. A few days later, someone entered her room and took from the bureau drawer the exact amount the dinner would have cost.

The law always stands back of the person who spends fearlessly with wisdom. For example, one of my students was shopping with her young nephew. The child clamored for a toy, which she told him she could not afford to buy. She realized suddenly that she was seeking lack and not recognizing God as her supply, so she bought the toy, and on her way home, picked up in the street the exact amount of money she had paid for it.

Our supply is inexhaustible and unfailing when fully trusted, but faith or trust must precede the demonstration. Jesus said, *"According to your faith be it unto you"* (Matthew 9:29 KJV). Faith is the substance of things hoped for and the evidence of things not seen, for faith holds the vision steady, and the adverse pictures are dissolved and dissipated, and in due season, we shall reap, if we faint not (see Hebrews 11:1; Galatians 6:9 KJV).

# DECREE
## AND
# AFFIRMATION

*I decree that it is dangerous to stop
in the middle of a hunch.*

*I affirm that the Holy Spirit is never too late.*

# 54

# Hope Chest

I n my classes, I often emphasize the importance of digging ditches or preparing for the things asked for, which shows active faith and brings the demonstration to pass.

A man in my class, whom I called the life of the party because he always tried to find a question I couldn't answer, but he never succeeded, asked, "Why is it then, that a lot of women who prepare hope chests never get married?"

I replied, "Because it is a *hope* chest, not a *faith* chest."

The prospective bride also violates law in telling others about it. Her friends come in and sit on the hope chest and they either doubt or hope together. Rather, "*...pray to your Father in private. Then your Father, who sees everything, will reward you*" (Matthew 6:6 NLT).

The student should never talk of a demonstration until it has jelled or comes to pass on the external. So a hope chest should become a faith chest and be kept from the public eye and the words spoken for the divine selection of a husband under grace in a perfect way. Those whom God have joined together, no thought can put asunder.

# DECREE

## AND

# AFFIRMATION

*I decree that hope looks forward.*

*I affirm that faith knows it has already received and acts accordingly.*

# 55

# Under Grace

J esus Christ brought the good news, the Gospel, that there was a higher law than the law of karma and that law transcends the law of karma. It is the law of grace, or forgiveness. It is the law that frees us from the law of cause and effect, the law of consequence. On this plane, we reap where we have not sown. The gifts of God are simply poured out upon us. This continued state of bliss awaits the one who has overcome worldly thoughts. In the world thought, there is tribulation, but as Jesus Christ said, *"Be of good cheer. I have overcome the world"* (John 16:33 NKJV). The world thought is that of sin, sickness, and death. Jesus saw the people's absolute unreality and said that sickness and sorrow shall pass away, and death itself, the last enemy, will be overcome (see 1 Corinthians 15:26; Revelation 21:4).

We know now, from a scientific standpoint, that death could be overcome by stamping the subconscious mind with the conviction of eternal youth and eternal life. The subconscious, being simply power without direction, carries out orders without questioning. Working under the direction of the superconscious, the Christ or God within us, the resurrection of the body would be accomplished. Humankind would no longer throw off the body in death. It would be transformed into the body electric—sung by Walt Whitman, for Christianity is founded upon the forgiveness of sins and an empty tomb.

# DECREE
## AND
# AFFIRMATION

*I decree that every plan my Father in Heaven has not planned is dissolved and obliterated and the divine design of my life now comes to pass.*

*I affirm that what God has given me can never be taken from me, for His gifts are for all eternity.*

# 56

# Lighten Your Burden

When we know our own powers and the workings of our mind, our great desire is to find an easy and quick way to impress the subconscious with good, for simply an intellectual knowledge of the Truth will not bring results.

In my own case, I've found the easiest way is in casting the burden. A metaphysician once explained it in this manner. He said, "The only thing that gives anything weight in nature is the law of gravitation, and if a boulder could be taken high above the planet, there would be no weight in that boulder." That is what Jesus Christ meant when He said, *"My yoke is easy and my burden is light."* He had overcome the world vibration and functioned in the fourth dimensional realm, where there is only perfection, completion, life and joy.

We are also told in Psalm 55:22, to *"Cast your burden on the Lord."* Many passages in the Bible state that the battle is God's, not ours, and that we are always to *"stand still"* and see the salvation of the Lord. This indicates that the superconscious mind, or Christ within, is where He fights our battles and relieves us of burdens. We violate that law if we carry a burden. A burden is an adverse thought or condition that has its root in the subconscious.

It seems almost impossible to make any headway directing the subconscious from the conscious or reasoning mind as the reasoning mind, the intellect, is limited in its conceptions, and filled with doubts and fears. How scientific is it then, to cast the burden upon the superconscious mind, or Christ within, where it is made light, or dissolved into its native nothingness.

# DECREE

## AND

# AFFIRMATION

*I decree that Christ within is the light within me.*

*I affirm that all doubt and fear
is consumed by His light.*

# 57

# I Go Free

A woman in urgent need of money called upon the Christ within, the superconscious, with the statement, "I cast this burden of lack on the Christ within and I go free to have plenty." The belief in lack was her burden; as she cast it upon the superconscious with its belief of plenty, an avalanche of supply was the result. We read in Colossians 1:27, "*The Christ in you, the hope of glory.*"

Another example. One of my students had been given a new piano, and there was no room in her studio for it until she had moved out the old one. She was in a state of perplexity. She wanted to keep the old piano, but knew of no place to send it. She became desperate, as the new piano was to be sent immediately. In fact, it was on its way, with no place to put it. She said it came to her to repeat, "I cast this burden on the Christ within, and I go free." A few moments later, her phone rang, and a woman friend asked if she might rent her old piano, and it was moved out a few minutes before the new one arrived.

I knew a woman, whose burden was resentment. She said, "I cast this burden of resentment on the Christ within, and I go free to be loving, harmonious, and happy." The almighty super-conscious flooded the subconscious with love and her whole life was changed. For years, resentment had held her in a state of torment and imprisoned her soul, the subconscious mind.

The statement should be made over and over and over, sometimes for hours at a time, silently or audibly, with quietness but determination. I have often compared it to winding up a Victrola. We must wind ourselves up with positive spoken words.

# DECREE
## AND
# AFFIRMATION

*I decree that God utilizes every person and every situation to bring me my heart's desires.*

*I affirm that hindrances are friendly and obstacles springboards. I now jump into my good.*

# 58

# The Manifestation of Good

I have noticed, in casting the burden, after a little while, we see clearly. It is impossible to have clear vision while in the throes of the carnal mind. Doubts and fear poison the mind and body, and imagination runs riot, attracting disaster and disease. In steadily repeating the affirmation, "I cast this burden on the Christ within and go free," the vision clears, and with it a feeling of relief, and sooner or later comes the manifestation of good, be it health, happiness, or supply.

One of my students once asked me to explain the darkness before the dawn. Previously I referred to the fact that often before a big demonstration, everything seems to go wrong, and deep depression clouds the consciousness. It means that out of the subconscious are rising the doubts and fears of the ages. These old derelicts of the subconscious rise to the surface to be put out.

Then is when we should clap our cymbals, like Jehoshaphat, and give thanks that we are saved, even though we seem surrounded by the enemy, the situation of lack or disease. The student continued, "How long must one remain in the dark?"

I replied, "Until we can see in the dark, and casting the burden enables us to see in the dark."

# DECREE

## AND

# AFFIRMATION

*I decree seeing my good in a golden glow of glory.*

*I affirm seeing my field shining
white with the harvest.*

# 59

# Believe

To impress the subconscious, active faith is always essential. Faith without works is dead. I have endeavored to bring out these points. Jesus Christ showed active faith when He commanded the multitude to sit down on the ground before He gave thanks for the loaves and the fishes. I will give another example showing how necessary this step is. In fact, active faith is the bridge over which we pass to our promised land.

Through a misunderstanding, a woman had been separated from her husband, whom she loved deeply. He refused all offers of reconciliation and would not communicate with her in any way. Coming into the knowledge of Spiritual Law, she denied the appearance of separation. She made this statement, "There is no separation in God's divine mind. Therefore, I cannot be separated from the love and companionship that are mine by divine right."

She showed active faith by arranging a place for him at the table every day, thereby impressing the subconscious with a picture of his return. Over a year passed, but she never wavered, and one day he walked in.

# DECREE

## AND

# AFFIRMATION

*I decree that God is my unfailing and immediate supply of all good.*

*I affirm that I am powerful and poised to receive.*

# 60

# With Music and Dancing

The subconscious is often impressed through music. Music has a fourth dimensional quality and releases the soul from imprisonment. It makes wonderful things seem possible, and easy to accomplish. I have a friend who uses music, daily, for this purpose. It puts her in perfect harmony and releases the imagination. Another woman often dances while making her affirmations. The rhythm and harmony of music and motion carry her words forth with tremendous power.

The student must remember also not to despise the day of small things. Invariably, before a demonstration, come signs of land. Before Columbus reached America, he saw birds and twigs, which showed him land was near. So it is with a demonstration, but often the student mistakes it for the demonstration itself and is disappointed.

For example, a woman had spoken the word for a set of dishes. Not long afterward, a friend gave her a dish which was old and cracked. She came to me and said, "Well, I asked for a set of dishes, and all I got was a cracked plate." I replied, "The plate was only signs of land. It shows your dishes are coming.

Look upon it as a birds and seaweed," and not long afterward the dishes came.

Continually making believe impresses the subconscious. If you make believe you are rich and successful, in due time you will reap. Children are always making believe, and as Jesus said, *"unless you turn from your sins and become like little children, you will never get into the Kingdom of Heaven"* (Matthew 18:3 NLT).

# DECREE
## AND
# AFFIRMATION

*I decree that my greatest expectations*
*are realized in a miraculous way.*

*I affirm that I water my wilderness with faith*
*and suddenly it blossoms as the rose.*

**61**

# Choose Whom You Will Serve

There is no peace or happiness for us until we have erased all fear from the subconscious. Fear is misdirected energy and must be redirected or transmuted into faith. Jesus Christ said, *"Why are ye fearful, oh ye of little faith?"* (Matthew 8:26 KJV). After all, *"...all things are possible to him who believes"* (Mark 9:23 NKJV).

I am asked so often by my students, "How can I get rid of fear?"

I reply, "By walking up to the thing you are afraid of." The lion takes its fierceness from your fear. Walk up to the lion, and he will disappear. Run away, and he runs after you.

Many of my students have come out of the bondage of poverty and are now bountifully supplied, through losing all fear of letting money go out. The subconscious is impressed with the truth that God is the Giver and Gift. Therefore, as one is one with the Giver, you are one with the Gift. A splendid statement is, "I now thank God the Giver for God the Gift."

Humankind has so long separated ourselves from God's good and His supply through thoughts of separation and lack, that sometimes it takes dynamite to dislodge these false ideas from our subconscious, and the dynamite is a big situation. We must watch ourselves hourly to detect if our motive for action is fear or faith. Choose this day whom you shall serve, fear or faith.

# DECREE
## AND
# AFFIRMATION

*I decree that God's plans for me are built upon a solid rock, I shall not fear.*

*I affirm that fear and poverty have no place in my thought life—only the God of truth and freedom will I serve.*

# 62

# Vain Imaginations

Perhaps your fear is of someone's personality. If so, don't avoid the people feared. Be willing to meet them cheerfully, and they will either prove golden links in the chain of your good, or they will disappear harmoniously from your path.

Perhaps your fear is of disease or germs. Then be fearless and undisturbed in a germ-laden situation, and you will be immune. You can only contract germs while vibrating at the same rate as the germ, and fear drags people down to the level of the germ. Of course, the disease-laden germ is the product of carnal mind, as all thought must objectify. Germs do not exist in the superconscious or divine mind, therefore are the product of our own vain imagination.

In the twinkling of an eye, our release will come when we realize there is no power in evil. The material world will fade away, and the fourth dimensional world, the world of the wondrous, will swing into manifestation. And I saw a new Heaven, and a new Earth, and there shall be no more death, neither sorrow nor crying, neither shall there be any more pain, for the former things are passed away (see Revelation 21:1-4).

# DECREE
## AND
# AFFIRMATION

*I decree that nothing can defeat God.*

*I affirm, therefore, that nothing can defeat me.*

# 63

# Real Love

Pure, unselfish love draws to itself its own. It does not need to seek or demand. Scarcely anyone has the faintest conception of real love. Humans are selfish, tyrannical or fearful in affections, thereby losing love. Jealousy is the worst enemy of love, for the imagination runs riot, seeing the loved one attracted to another, and invariably these fears objectify if they are not neutralized.

For example, a woman came to me in deep distress. The man she loved had left her for other woman, and said he never intended to marry her. She was torn with jealousy and resentment, and said she hoped he would suffer as he had made her suffer, and added, "How could he leave me when I loved him so much?"

I replied, "You are not loving that man. You are hating him," and added, "You can never receive what you have never given. Give a perfect love and you will receive a perfect love. Perfect yourself on this man. Give him a perfect, unselfish love, demanding nothing in return, do not criticize or condemn, and bless him wherever he is."

She replied that she wouldn't bless him unless she knew where he was. "Well," I said, "that is not real love. When you send out real love, real love will return to you, either from this man or his equivalent, for if this man is not the divine selection, you will not want him. As you are one with God, you are one with the love that belongs to you by divine right."

Several months passed and she was working conscientiously within herself. She was becoming more poised, and gradually lost her resentment. He was a Captain, and she called him the Cap. One day she said suddenly, "God bless the Cap wherever he is."

After a few weeks, I received a letter saying, "We're married!" At the earliest opportunity, I paid her a call. My first words were, "What happened?"

"Oh," she exclaimed, "a miracle. One day I woke up, and all suffering had ceased. I saw him that evening and he asked me to marry him. We were married in about a week, and I have never seen a more devoted man."

# DECREE

## AND

# AFFIRMATION

*I decree that I wait patiently on the Lord.*

*I affirm that I trust in Him.*

# 64

# Love Your Work

No one is a success in business unless they loves their work. The picture the artist paints for the love of art is the greatest work. No one can attract money if they despise it. Many people are kept in poverty by saying, "Money means nothing to me. I have a contempt for people who have it." This is the reason so many artists are poor. Their contempt for money separates them from it. I remember hearing one artist say of another, "He's no good as an artist, but he has money in the bank." This attitude of mind, of course, separates us from our supply. We must be in harmony with what we want to attract.

Money is God in manifestation, as freedom from want and limitation; but it must be always kept in circulation and put to right uses. Hoarding and saving react with grim vengeance. This does not mean that we should not have houses and lots, stocks and bonds, for the barns of the righteous shall be full (see Psalm 144:13). It means we should not hoard even the principal if an occasion arises when money is necessary. In letting it go out fearlessly and cheerfully, we open the way for more to come in, for God is our unfailing and inexhaustible supply. This is the spiritual attitude toward money, and the great Bank of the Universal never fails.

# DECREE

## AND

# AFFIRMATION

*I decree that I now have the fearless
faith of the Christ within.*

*I affirm that at my approach, barriers
vanish and obstacles disappear.*

# 65

# No Hoarding Allowed

We see an example of hoarding in the film production of *Greed*. The woman won $5,000 in a lottery but would not spend it. She hoarded and saved, let her husband suffer and starve, and eventually, she scrubbed floors for a living. She loved the money itself and put it above everything—and one night she was murdered and the money taken from her. This is an example of where love of money is the root of all evil. Money in itself is good and beneficial, but used for destructive purposes, hoarded and saved, or considered more important than love, brings disease and disaster, and the loss of the money itself.

Follow the path of love, and all things are added, for God is love, and God is supply. Follow the path of selfishness and greed, and the supply vanishes.

For example, I knew the case of a very rich woman who hoarded her income. She rarely gave anything away, but bought and bought and bought things for herself. She was very fond of necklaces, and a friend once asked her how many she possessed. She replied, "Sixty-seven." She bought them and put them away, carefully wrapped in tissue paper. Had she used the necklaces, it would have been quite legitimate, but she was violating the law of use. Her closets were filled with clothes she never wore and jewels that never saw the light of day.

The old woman's arms were gradually becoming paralyzed from holding on to things, and eventually she was considered incapable of looking after her affairs and her wealth was handed over to others to manage.

# DECREE

## AND

# AFFIRMATION

*I decree that all fear is now banished in the name of Jesus Christ, for I know there is no power to hurt me.*

*I affirm that God is the one and only Power.*

# 66

# Self-Destruction Versus Love

In ignorance of the law, we bring about our own destruction. All disease, all unhappiness come from the violation of the law of love. Our boomerangs of hate, resentment, and criticism return to us laden with sickness and sorrow. Love seems almost a lost art, but the person with the knowledge of Spiritual Law knows it must be regained, for without it, we become as *"a noisy gong or a clanging cymbal"* (1 Corinthians 13:1 NLT).

For example, I had a student who came to me, month after month, to clean her consciousness of resentment. After a while, she arrived at the point where she resented only one woman, but that one woman kept her busy. Little by little she became poised and harmonious, and one day, all resentment was wiped out.

She came in radiant and exclaimed, "You can't understand how I feel. The woman said something to me and instead of being furious, I was loving and kind, and she apologized and was perfectly lovely to me. No one can understand the marvelous lightness I feel within."

# DECREE

## AND

# AFFIRMATION

*I decree that I am in perfect harmony with God, for He knows nothing of obstacles, time or space—only completion.*

*I affirm that God works in unexpected ways, His wonders to perform.*

# 67

# Fear Not

I knew a woman who went about bragging of her troubles, so of course she always had something to brag about. The old idea was if a woman did not worry about her children, she was not a good mother. Now we know that mother-fear is responsible for many of the diseases and accidents that come into the lives of children, for fear pictures vividly the disease or situation feared, and these pictures objectify if not neutralized. Happy is the mother who can say sincerely that she puts her child in God's hands, and therefore knows that the child is divinely protected!

For example, a woman awoke suddenly in the night, feeling her brother was in great danger. Instead of giving in to her fears, she commenced making statements of truth, saying, "Man is a perfect idea in God's divine mind, and is always in his right place. Therefore, my brother is in his right place and is divinely protected." The next day, she found that her brother had been in close proximity to an explosion in a mine, but had miraculously escaped.

So we are our brother's keeper, in thought, and everyone should know that who we love dwells in the secret place of the most high, and abides under the shadow of the Almighty. No evil will befall them there, neither shall any plague come near their home. Perfect love casts out fear. Whoever fears is not made perfect in love, and love is the fulfilling of the law.

# DECREE

## AND

# AFFIRMATION

*I decree that my ditches are dug deep with faith and understanding and my heart's desire comes to pass in a surprising way.*

*I affirm that my ditches will be filled at the right time, bringing all that I have asked for and more.*

# 68

# Ask and Receive

I have often been asked just how to make a demonstration of receiving what you ask for. I reply, "Speak the word and then do not do anything until you get a definite lead. Demand the lead, saying, 'Infinite Spirit, reveal to me the way. Let me know if there's anything for me to do." The answer will come through intuition, or hunch, a chance remark from someone, or a passage in a book, etc. The answers are sometimes quite startling in their exactness.

For example, a woman desired a large sum of money. She spoke the words, "Infinite Spirit, open the way for my immediate supply. Let all that is mine by divine right now reach me in great avalanches of abundance." Then she added, "Give me a definite lead. Let me know if there is anything for me to do."

The thought came quickly to her, "Give a certain friend one hundred dollars." This friend had helped her spiritually. She told her friend, who said, "Wait and get another lead before giving it." So she waited, and that day met a woman who said to her, "I gave someone a dollar today. It was just as much for me as it would be for you to give someone one hundred dollars." This was indeed an unmistakable lead, so the woman knew she was right in giving the $100. It was a gift that proved a great investment, for shortly after that, a large sum of money came to her in a remarkable way.

# DECREE

## AND

# AFFIRMATION

*I decree and give thanks that I now receive the righteous desires of my heart.*

*I affirm that mountains are removed, valleys exalted and every crooked place made straight.*

# 69

# Giving and Receiving

Giving opens the way for receiving. To create activity in finances, we should give. Tithing, or giving one tenth of our income, is an old Jewish custom and sure to bring increase. Many of the richest men in this country have been tithers and have never known it to fail as an investment. The tenth part goes forth and returns blessed and multiplied—but the gift or tithe must be given with love and cheerfulness, for God loveth a cheerful giver (2 Corinthians 9:7).

Bills should be paid cheerfully. All money should be sent forth fearlessly and with a blessing. This attitude of mind makes you the master of your money. Your spoken word then opens vast reservoirs of wealth. You limit your supply by limited vision. Sometimes the student has a great realization of wealth, but is afraid to act. The vision and action must go hand in hand, as in the case of the man who bought the fur-lined overcoat.

One day a woman asked me to speak the word for a certain job, so I demanded, "Infinite Spirit, open the way for this woman's right position." Never ask for just "a" position. Ask for the right position, the place already planned in God's divine mind, as it is the only one that will give satisfaction. I then gave thanks that she had already received, and that it would manifest quickly.

Very soon, she had three positions offered her, two in New York and one in Palm Beach, and she didn't know which to choose. I said, "Ask for a definite lead." The time was almost up and was still undecided when one day, she telephoned and told me, "When I woke up this morning, I could smell Palm Beach." She had been there before and knew its balmy fragrance.

I replied, "Well, if you can smell Palm Beach from here, it's certainly your lead." She accepted the position, and it proved a great success. Often, a lead comes in an unexpected way.

# DECREE

## AND

# AFFIRMATION

*I decree that I'm in the Kingdom of fulfillment.*

*I affirm that I have perfect confidence in God and God has perfect confidence in me.*

# 70

# Intuition

One day, I was walking down the street when I suddenly felt a strong urge to go to a certain bakery a block or two away. The reasoning mind resisted, arguing, "There is nothing there that you want." However, I had learned not to reason, so I went to the bakery, looked at everything, and there was certainly nothing there that I wanted.

But coming out, I encountered a woman I had thought of often and who was in great need of the help that I could give her.

So often, we go for one thing and find another. Intuition is a spiritual faculty and does not explain but simply points the way. A person often receives a lead during a time of confusion. The idea that comes may seem quite irrelevant, but some of God's leadings are mysterious.

# DECREE

## AND

# AFFIRMATION

*I decree that with God, all things are easy and possible now. I stand aside and watch God work.*

*I affirm how it interests me to see how quickly and easily He brings the desires of my heart to pass.*

# 71

# Congestion

In class one day, I told the students that each individual would receive a definite lead. A woman came to me afterward and said, "While you were treating, I got the hunch to take my furniture out of storage and get an apartment." The woman had come to be treated for health.

I told her I knew in getting a home of her own, her health would improve, and I added, "I believe your trouble, which is a congestion, has come from having things stored away. Congestion of things causes congestion in the body. You have violated the law of use, and your body is paying the penalty," so I gave thanks that divine order was established in her mind, body, and affairs.

People seldom think of how their affairs react on the body. I believe there is a mental correspondence for every disease. A person might receive instantaneous healing through the realization of his or her body being a perfect idea in God's divine mind, and therefore whole and perfect. But if individuals continue their destructive thinking, hoarding, hating, fearing, condemning, the disease will return (see Matthew 12:43-45 NLT).

# DECREE

## AND

# AFFIRMATION

*I decree that I now put to flight the army
of the aliens or negative thoughts.*

*I affirm that they feed on fear and starve on faith.*

# 72

# Permanent Healing

Our soul, or subconscious mind, must be washed whiter than snow for permanent healing, and the metaphysician is always delving deep for the reasoning. Jesus Christ said, *"Judge not, and ye shall not be judged: condemn not, and ye shall not be condemned"* (Luke 6:37 KJV). Many people have attracted disease and unhappiness through judgment and condemnation of others. What we condemn in others, we attract to ourselves!

For example, a friend came to me in anger and distress because her husband had deserted her for another woman. She condemned the other woman and said continually, "She knew he was a married man. She had no right to accept his attentions."

I replied, "Stop condemning the woman. Bless her and be through with the situation. Otherwise, you are attracting the same thing to yourself." She was deaf to my words, and a year or two later became deeply interested in a married man, herself. We pick up a live hot wire whenever we criticize or condemn—and we may expect a shock!

# DECREE

## AND

# AFFIRMATION

*I decree that judgment and condemnation have no place in my thoughts, words, or actions.*

*I affirm that what I think, say, and do will attract similar responses from others.*

# 73

# Indecision, a Stumbling Block

Indecision is a stumbling block in many people's pathway. To overcome it, make the statement repeatedly, "I am always under direct inspiration. I make right decisions, quickly." These words impress the subconscious, and soon we find ourselves awake and alert, making right moves without hesitation. I have found it destructive to look to the psychic plane for guidance, as it is the plane of many minds and not the One divine mind.

As we open our mind to subjectivity, we become a target for destructive forces. The psychic plane is the result of human mortal thought, and is on the plane of opposites. We may receive either good or bad messages. The science of numbers and the reading of horoscopes keep people down on the mental or mortal plane, for they deal only with the karmic path. I know of a man who should have been dead years ago according to his horoscope, but he is alive and a leader of one of the biggest movements in this country for the uplift of humanity.

It takes a very strong mind to neutralize a prophecy of evil. The student should declare, "Every false prophecy shall come to naught. Every plan my Father in Heaven has not planned shall be dissolved and dissipated. His divine idea now comes to pass." Our will should back the universal will of God. I will that the will of God be done.

# DECREE

## AND

# AFFIRMATION

*I decree that my good is a perfect and permanent idea His divine mind and must manifest, for there is nothing to prevent.*

*I affirm and cast every burden on the Christ within and I go free.*

# 74

# Lost and Found

When we lose something, it shows there is a belief of loss in our subconscious mind. As we erases this false belief, the article or its equivalent will appear on the external. For example, a woman lost a silver pencil in a theater. She made every effort to find it but it was not returned. She denied loss, taking the affirmation, "I deny loss. There is no loss in divine mind. Therefore I cannot lose that pencil. I will receive it or its equivalent."

Several weeks elapsed. One day she was with a friend who wore about her neck on a cord a beautiful gold pencil who turned to her and said, "Do you want this pencil? I paid $50 for it at Tiffany's."

The woman was aghast and replied, almost forgetting to thank her friend, "Oh God, aren't You wonderful? The silver pencil wasn't good enough for me."

We can only lose what doesn't belong to us by divine right or isn't good enough for us. There is no loss in God's divine mind. Therefore, I cannot lose anything that is rightfully mine.

Infinite Intelligence is never too late. Infinite Intelligence knows the way of recovery. There is no loss in His divine mind. Therefore, I cannot lose anything that belongs to me. It will be restored or I will receive its equivalent.

# DECREE

## AND

# AFFIRMATION

*I decree that I can only lose what doesn't belong to me by divine right or isn't good enough for me.*

*I affirm that there is no loss in God's divine mind. Therefore, I cannot lose anything that is rightfully mine.*

# 75

# No Debt

If a man is in debt or people owe him money, it shows that a belief of debt is in his subconscious mind. This belief must be neutralized to change conditions. For example, a woman came to me saying a man had owed her $1000 for years, which she could not compel him to pay.

I said, "You must work on yourself, not the man," and gave her this statement, "I deny debt. There is no debt in God's divine mind. No one owes me anything. All is squared. I send that man love and forgiveness." In a few weeks, she received a letter from him saying he intended sending the money, and in about a month came the $1000.

If the student owes money, change the statement: "There is no debt in the divine mind. Therefore, I owe no one anything. All is squared. All my obligations are now wiped out under grace in a perfect way. I deny debt. There is no debt in divine mind. Therefore, I owe no man anything. All obligations are now wiped out under grace. In a miraculous way, I deny debt. There is no debt in divine mind. No man owes me anything. All is squared. I send forth love and forgiveness."

# DECREE

## AND

# AFFIRMATION

*I decree that there is no debt in God's divine mind. No one owes me anything.*

*I affirm that all is squared—God sends forth love and forgiveness.*

# 76

# Mountain-Moving Faith

A woman who lived in a country town wished to sell her house and furniture. It was in the winter with snow so deep it was almost impossible for cars or wagons to reach her door. As she had asked God to sell her furniture to the right person for the right price, she was unmindful of appearances. She polished the furniture, pushed it into the middle of the room and prepared to sell it.

She said, "I never looked out the window at the blizzard. I simply trusted God's promises." In miraculous ways, people drove up and all the furniture was sold, and the house also, without paying any commission to an agent.

Faith never looks out of the window at the blizzard, it simply prepares for the blessing asked for.

# DECREE

## AND

# AFFIRMATION

*I decree that God will provide for perfect satisfaction.*

*I affirm that faith never looks out of the window at the blizzard, it simply prepares for the blessing asked for.*

# 77

# An Effort of the Will

It is God's will to give believers every righteous desire of their heart, and our will should be used to hold that perfect vision, without wavering. The prodigal son said, "I will arise and go to my father." It is indeed often an effort of the will to leave the husks and swine of mortal thinking. It is so much easier for the average person to have fear than faith—so faith is an effort of the will.

As we become spiritually awakened, we recognize that any external inharmony is the result of mental inharmony. If we stumble or fall, we may know we are stumbling or falling in consciousness.

One day a student was walking along the street condemning someone in her thoughts. She was saying mentally, "That woman is the most disagreeable woman on earth," when suddenly three Boy Scouts rushed around the corner and almost knocked her over. She did not condemn the Boy Scouts; rather, she immediately called on the law of forgiveness and saluted the divinity in the woman. Wisdom's way are ways of pleasantness and all her paths are peace (see Proverbs 3:17).

# DECREE

## AND

# AFFIRMATION

*I decree that I am identified in
love with the Spirit of God.*

*I affirm that God protects my interests and His
divine idea now comes out of every situation.*

# 78

# Will It Ever Clear Up?

Always on our pathway is our message or lead. For example, a woman was much troubled over an unhappy situation. She thought to herself, *Will it ever clear up?*

Her maid was standing near and commenced to tell her of her experiences. The woman was too worried to be interested but listened patiently. The maid was saying, "I worked in a hotel once where there was a very amusing gardener. He always said such funny things. It had been raining for three days and I said to him, 'Do you think it will ever clear up?' And he replied, 'My God, doesn't it always clear up?'"

The woman was amazed. It was the answer to her thoughts. She said, reverently, "Yes. With my God, it always clears up." Soon after, her problem did clear up in an unexpected way.

# DECREE

## AND

# AFFIRMATION

*I decree that I am always under direct inspiration and know just what to do. I give instant obedience to my intuitive leads.*

*I affirm my angel of destiny goes before me, keeping me in the way.*

# 79

# Surprises!

When we have made demands upon the Universal One, we must be ready for surprises. Everything may seem to be going wrong, when in reality it is going right. For example, a woman was told that there was no loss in God's divine mind, therefore she could not lose anything that belonged to her. Anything lost would be returned, or she would receive its equivalent.

Several years previously, she had lost $2,000. She had loaned the money to a relative during her lifetime, but the relative had died, leaving no mention of it in her will. The woman was resentful and angry, and as she had no written statement of the transaction, she never received the money, so she determined to deny the loss, and collect the $2,000 from the Bank of the Universal.

She had to begin by forgiving the woman, as resentment and unforgiveness close the doors of this wonderful bank. She made this statement, "I deny loss, there is no loss in His divine mind. Therefore, I cannot lose the $2,000 that belong to me by divine right." As one door shuts another door opens. She was living in an apartment house that was for sale, and in the lease was a clause stating that if the house was sold, the tenants would be required to move out within 90 days. Suddenly, the landlord broke the leases and raised the rent.

Again, injustice was on her pathway, but this time she was undisturbed. She blessed the landlord and said, "As the rent has been raised, it means that I'll be that much richer, for God is my supply." The new leases were made out for the advanced rent, but by some divine mistake, the 90-day clause had been forgotten. Soon after, the landlord had an opportunity to sell the house.

On account of the mistake in the new leases, the tenants held possession for another year. The agent offered each tenant $200 to vacate. Several families moved. Three remained, including the woman. A month or two passed, and the agent again appeared. This time he said to the woman, "Will you break your lease for the sum of $1,500?"

It flashed upon her, *Here comes the $2,000.* She remembered having said to friends in the house, "We will all act together if anything more is said about leaving," so her lead was to consult her friends.

These friends said," Well, if they have offered you $1,500, they will certainly give $2,000," so she received a check for $2,000 for giving up the apartment. It was certainly a remarkable working of the law, and the apparent injustice was merely opening the way for her to regain the money. It proved that there is no loss, and when we take a spiritual stand, we collect all that is ours from His great reservoir of good.

# DECREE

## AND

# AFFIRMATION

*I decree all power is given to me to
be meek and lowly of heart.*

*I affirm I am willing to come last.*

# WHEN WE

## HAVE MADE

# DEMANDS

## UPON THE

## *Universal One,*

## WE MUST

# BE READY

## FOR

## *surprises.*

# 80

# Pour Out a Blessing

God says He will restore to us the years the locusts have eaten (Joel 2:25). The locusts are the doubts, fears, resentments, and regrets of mortal thinking. These adverse thoughts rob us of our peace of mind. We are here to prove God and to bear witness to the truth, and He can only prove Himself by bringing plenty out of lack, and justice out of justice (see Malachi 3:10).

No wind can drive my bark astray, nor change the tide of destiny. There is for each person perfect self-expression. There is a place we are to fill and no one else can fill, something we are to do that no one else can do. It is our destiny. This achievement is held, a perfect idea in divine mind, awaiting our recognition. As the imaging faculty is the creative faculty, it is necessary for us to see the idea before it can manifest, so our highest demand is for the divine design of our life. We may not have the faintest conception of what it is, for there is possibly some marvelous talent hidden deep within. Our demand should be, "Infinite Spirit, open the way for the divine design of my life to manifest. Let the genius within me now be released. Let me see clearly the perfect plan."

The perfect plan includes health, wealth, love, and perfect self-expression. This is the square of life that brings perfect happiness. When we have made this demand, we may find great changes taking place in our life, for nearly every person has wandered far from the divine design.

In one woman's case, it was as though a cyclone had struck her affairs, but readjustments came quickly, and new and wonderful conditions took the place of old ones. Perfect self-expression will never be labor, but of such absorbing interest that it will seem almost like play. The student knows, also, as we come into the world financed by God, the supply needed for our perfect self-expression will be at hand.

# DECREE

## AND

# AFFIRMATION

*I decree to now place my personal will upon the altar: Your will, not my will; Your way, not my way; Your time, not my time.*

*I affirm that in the twinkling of an eye, it is done.*

# 81

# Perfect Divine Design

Many a genius has struggled for years with the problem of supply, when his spoken word and faith would have released quickly the necessary funds. For example, after class one day, a man came to me and handed me a cent. He said, "I have just seven cents in the world, and I'm going to give you one, for I have faith in the power of your spoken word. I want you to speak the word for my perfect self-expression and prosperity."

I spoke the word and did not see him again until a year later. He came in one day, successful and happy, with a roll of bills in a pocket. He said, "Immediately after you spoke the word, I had a position offered me in a distant city and am now demonstrating health, happiness, and supply."

Demand definite leads, and the way will be made easy and successful. We should not visualize or force a mental picture. When we demand the divine design to come into our conscious minds, we will receive flashes of inspiration and begin to see ourselves making some great accomplishment. This is the picture or idea we must hold without wavering.

What we seek is seeking us. As such, the telephone was seeking Alexander Graham Bell.

# DECREE

## AND

# AFFIRMATION

*I decree that there are no mysteries in the Kingdom. Whatever I shall know will now be revealed to me under grace.*

*I affirm that I'm a perfect, non-resistant instrument for God to work through and His perfect plan for me now comes to pass.*

# 82

# The Science of the Mind

P arents should never force careers and professions upon their children. With a knowledge of spiritual truth, the divine plan could be spoken for early in childhood, or even prenatally. A prenatal treatment should be, "Let the God in this child have perfect expression. Let the divine design of this child's mind, body, and affairs be made manifest throughout life, throughout eternity."

God's will be done, not human will. God's pattern, not human pattern, is the command we find running throughout the Scriptures. The Bible deals with the science of the mind. God's Word tells us how to release our soul, or subconscious mind, from bondage. The battles described are of humans waging war against mortal thoughts. Our foes are within our own minds. We must be careful that we are not the wicked and slothful servant who buried his talent. There is a terrible penalty to be paid for not using one's ability (see Matthew 25:29-30).

Often, fear stands between us and our perfect self-expression. Stage fright has hampered many a genius. This may be overcome by the spoken word, or treatment. The individual then loses all self-consciousness and feels simply that we are channels for the Infinite Intelligence to use. We are under direct inspiration, fearless, and confident, for we know that the Father within is doing the work.

# DECREE
## AND
# AFFIRMATION

*I decree that I'm surrounded by the white light of the Christ through which nothing negative can penetrate.*

*I affirm walking in the light of Christ and my fear giants dwindle into nothingness.*

# 83

# In All Your Ways

A young boy came often to my class with his mother. He asked me to speak the word for his coming examinations at school. I told him to make the statement, "I am one with Infinite Intelligence. I know everything I should know on this subject." He had an excellent knowledge of history, but was not sure of his arithmetic. I saw him afterward, and he said, "I spoke the word for my arithmetic and passed with the highest honors, but I thought I could depend on myself for history and got a very poor mark." We often receive a setback when we are too sure of ourselves, which means we trust ourselves and wisdom rather than the Father within.

Another one of my students gave me an example of this. She took an extended trip abroad one summer, visiting many countries where she was unfamiliar with the languages. She was calling to Infinite Intelligence for guidance and protection every minute, and her affairs went smoothly and miraculously. Her luggage was never delayed nor lost, accommodations were always ready for her at the best hotels, and she had perfect service wherever she went. She returned to New York. Knowing the language, she felt God was longer necessary, so looked after her affairs in an ordinary manner. Everything went wrong, her trunks were delayed, amid inharmony and confusion.

The student must form the habit of practicing the presence of God every minute. In all thy ways acknowledge Him (see Proverbs 3:6). Nothing is too small or too great to turn unto Him.

# DECREE

## AND

# AFFIRMATION

*I decree that God's divine mind is ready and able to handle all of my asks.*

*I affirm that His protection and guidance are awaiting my requests.*

# 84

# A Supply for Every Demand

There is a divine design for each person. Just as the perfect picture of the oak tree is in the acorn, the divine pattern of a person's life is in the superconscious mind of that man or woman. In God's divine design, there is no limitation, only health, wealth, love and perfect self-expression.

On our pathway, there is always a divine selection. Each day we must live according to the divine plan or have unhappy reactions. For example, a woman moved into a new apartment which she had almost furnished when the thought came to her, *On that side of the room should stand a Chinese cabinet.*

Not long after, she was walking by an antique shop. She glanced in and there stood a magnificent Chinese cabinet about eight feet high, elaborately carved. She entered and asked the price. The salesman said it was worth $1000, but the woman who owned it was willing to take less. The man added, "What will you offer for it?"

The woman paused and the price $200 came into her mind, so she answered $200. The man said he would let her know if the offer was satisfactory. She did not want to cheat anyone or get anything that was not rightfully hers, so going home, she said repeatedly, "If it's mine, I can't lose it, and if it's not mine, I don't want it."

It was a snowy day and she said she emphasized her words by kicking the snow from right to left, clearing a pathway to her apartment. Several days elapsed when she was notified that the woman was willing to sell the cabinet for $200.

There is a supply for every demand—from Chinese cabinets to millions of dollars. Before you call, God will answer. But unless it is a divinely selected cabinet or millions, neither will ever bring happiness.

# DECREE

## AND

# AFFIRMATION

*I decree that I now do the things which*
*I can do and no one else can do.*

*I affirm that I'm fully equipped for the divine plan*
*of my life. I am more than equal to the situation.*

# 85

# A Matter of Consciousness

Wealth is a matter of consciousness. The French have a legend giving an example of this. A poor man was walking along a road when he met a traveler, who stopped him and said, "My good friend, I see you are poor. Take this gold nugget, sell it, and you will be rich all your days." The man was overjoyed at his good fortune and took the nugget home. He immediately found work and became so prosperous that he did not sell the nugget.

Years passed, and he became a very rich man. One day he met a poor man on the road. He stopped him and said, "My good friend, I will give you this gold nugget, which, if you sell, will make you rich for life." The beggar took the nugget, had it valued, and found it was only brass. So we see, the first man became rich through feeling rich, thinking the nugget was gold.

Every person has within themselves a gold nugget. It is our consciousness of gold, of opulence, which brings riches into our life. In speaking our demands, we begin at our journey's end. That is, we declare what we have already received. Before ye call I shall answer (see Isaiah 65:24). Continually affirming establishes the belief in the subconscious. It would not be necessary to make an affirmation more than once for the person who has perfect faith. You should not plead or supplicate, but give thanks repeatedly, that you have already received.

# DECREE

## AND

# AFFIRMATION

*I decree that all my needs have been provided for—I have received all I need.*

*I affirm that I live in the Kingdom of eternal joy and absorbing interest.*

# 86

# Rejoice!

*The desert shall rejoice and blossom as the rose.* This rejoicing, which is yet in the desert, state of consciousness, opens the way for release. The Lord's Prayer is in the form of command and demand, "Give us this day our daily bread and forgive us our debts as we forgive our debtors," and ends in praise, "For thine is the kingdom, and the power, and the glory, forever. Amen." Prayer is command and demand, praise and thanksgiving. The student's work is in making himself believe that with God, *all things are possible.*

This is easy enough to state in the abstract, but a little more difficult when confronted with a problem. For example, it was necessary for a woman to demonstrate a large sum of money within a stated time. She knew she must do something to get a realization, for realization is manifestation, and she demanded a lead. She was walking through a department store when she saw a very beautiful pink enamel letter opener. She felt the pull toward it.

The thought came, *I haven't a paper cutter good enough to open letters containing large checks.* So she bought the letter opener, which the reasoning mind would have called an extravagance. When she held it in her hand, she had a flash of a picture of herself opening an envelope containing a large check, and within a few weeks, she received the money. The pink envelope opener was her bridge of active faith.

# DECREE

## AND

# AFFIRMATION

*I decree that I see God in every face.*
*I see good in every situation.*

*I affirm that I have the crystal clear*
*vision of the desert rejoicing.*

# 87

# Subconscious Power

Many stories are told of the power of the subconscious when directed in faith. For example, a man was spending the night in a farmhouse. The windows of the room had been nailed down, and in the middle of the night, he felt suffocated and made his way in the dark to the window. He could not open it, so he smashed the pane with his fist, drew in drafts of fine fresh air, and had a wonderful night's sleep. The next morning, he found he had smashed the glass of a bookcase and the window had remained closed during the whole night. He had supplied himself with oxygen, simply by his thought of oxygen.

When students start out to demonstrate the truth of Scripture, they should never turn back. The person who wavers shall not receive anything of the Lord. A student once made this wonderful statement, "When I asks the Father for anything, I put my foot down, and I say, 'Father, I'll take nothing less than I've asked for, but more.'" So we should never compromise. Having done all, stand. This is sometimes the most difficult time of demonstrating. The temptation comes to give up, to turn back, to compromise. Don't. Trust God.

# DECREE

## AND

# AFFIRMATION

*I decree that I look up and down and
all around knowing that my good comes
from the north, south, east and west.*

*I affirm that my eyes are God's eyes—
perfect and flawless—and have seen the
demonstration of His faithfulness.*

# 88

# Decreed and Manifested

All the good that is to be made manifest in our life is already an accomplished fact in God's divine mind, and is released through our recognition or spoken word, so we must be careful to decree that only the divine idea be made manifest. Too often we decree, through idle words, failure, or misfortune. It is therefore of the utmost importance to word our demands correctly.

If you desire a home, friend, position, or any other good thing, make the demand for the divine selection. For example, "Infinite Spirit, open the way for my right home, my right friend, my right position. I give thanks that it now manifests under grace in a perfect way." The latter part of the statement is most important.

For example, I knew a woman who demanded $1,000. Her daughter was injured and they received $1,000 indemnity, so it did not come in a perfect way. The demand should have been worded, "Infinite Spirit, I give thanks that the $1,000, which is mine by divine right, is now released and reaches me under grace in a perfect way."

As we grow in a financial consciousness, we should demand that the enormous sums of money, which are ours by divine right, reach us *under grace in perfect ways.* It is impossible for us to release more than we think is possible, for we are bound by the limited expectancies of the subconscious. We must enlarge our expectancies in order to receive in a larger way. We so often limits ourselves in our demands. For example, a student made the demand for $600 by a certain date. He did receive it, but heard afterward that he came very near receiving $1,000, but he was given just $600 as a result of his spoken word. We can limit God's divine design.

# DECREE
## AND
# AFFIRMATION

*I decree that I am growing daily in God's grace and wisdom and will enlarge my expectancies.*

*I affirm and give thanks for all my divine rights and accept them all gratefully.*

# 89

## Cheerful Receivers

Some people are cheerful givers, but bad receivers. They refuse gifts through pride or some negative reason, thereby blocking their channels, and invariably find themselves eventually with little or nothing.

For example, a woman who had given away a great deal of money had a gift offered her of several thousand dollars. She refused to take it, saying she didn't need it. Shortly after that, her finances were tied up, and she found herself in debt for that same amount.

We should receive gracefully. *"Freely you have received, freely give"* (Matthew 10:8 NKJV). There is always a perfect balance of giving and receiving; and though we should give without thinking of returns, we violate law if we don't accept the returns that come to us, for all gifts are from God—people are merely the channel.

A thought of lack should never be held over the giver. For example, when the man gave me one cent, I did not say, "Poor man. He can't afford to give me that." I saw him rich and prosperous, with his supply pouring in. It was this thought that brought it. If you have been a bad receiver, become a good one, take even a postage stamp if given to you, and open up God's channels for receiving. The Lord loves a cheerful receiver, as well as a cheerful giver.

# DECREE

## AND

# AFFIRMATION

*I decree that the light of the Christ now streams throughout my mind, body, and affairs.*

*I affirm clearly hearing the voice of glad tidings of personal joy and success.*

# 90

# Your Request Is Granted

When students try to force a demonstration through the reasoning mind, they bring it to a standstill. We should act only through intuition or definite leads. Rest in the Lord and wait patiently. Trust also in Him, and He will bring it to pass. I have seen Spiritual Law work in the most astonishing manner.

For example, a student stated that it was necessary for her to have $100 for the following day. It was a debt of vital importance which had to be met. I spoke the word, declaring that the Infinite Spirit was never too late, and that the supply was at hand.

That evening, she phoned me of the miracle. She said that the thought came to her to go to her safety deposit box at the bank to examine some papers. She looked over the papers and at the bottom of the box was a new $100 bill. She was astounded, and she said she knew she had never put it there, for she had gone through the papers many times. I believe it may have been a materialization, as Jesus Christ materialized the loaves and fishes (see Matthew 14:13-21).

The fields, ripe with the harvest, will at times manifest immediately, as in all of the miracles of Jesus Christ. There is a tremendous power alone in the name Jesus Christ—it stands for truth made manifest. He said, *"Whatsoever ye shall ask the Father in my name, he will give it you"* (John 16:23 KJV). The power of His name raises you into the fourth dimension, where you are freed from all ungodly influences, and you become unconditioned and absolute, as God Himself is unconditioned and absolute.

# DECREE

## AND

# AFFIRMATION

*I decree that my heart is a perfect idea in God's divine mind and is now in its right place, doing its right work. It is a happy heart, a fearless heart and a loving heart.*

*I affirm that the light of the Christ streams through my body and I give thanks for my radiant health and happiness.*

# Florence Scovel Shinn

Florence Scovel Shinn (1871-1940) was born in Camden, New Jersey, and is best known for her book *The Game of Life and How to Play It,* published in 1925, which she self-published. She wrote several other books and was also an accomplished pencil drawing illustrator. Her artwork appeared in numerous magazines and books including *Harper's* and popular novels.

Florence Scovel Shinn attended the Pennsylvania Academy of the Fine Arts in Philadelphia. She and her husband moved to New York where he wrote three plays in which his wife played a leading role. Later in life, during the early 19th century, she became known as a "New Thought spiritual teacher," in the company of writers such as Mary Baker Eddy, Phineas Quimby, and Charles Fillmore.

To train the imagination successfully, you must understand the workings of your mind. In Florence Scovel Shinn's classic work you will discover the secret to playing the game of life successfully. Beginning with the explanation of the functions of the three departments of the mind: the subconscious, conscious, and superconscious, the author offers the required knowledge and tools for beating your excuses to achieve breakthrough results in accumulating wealth and reaching your goals.

A must-read for anyone interested in the psychological tactics of becoming a stronger, more savvy version of yourself.

# THANK YOU FOR READING THIS BOOK!

If you found any of the information helpful, please take a few minutes and leave a review on the bookselling platform of your choice.

## BONUS GIFT!

Don't forget to sign up to try our newsletter and grab your free personal development ebook here:

soundwisdom.com/classics

Made in United States
Orlando, FL
23 January 2024

42822975R00115